Hereford

The Late Tudor and Early Stuart City and its People

by

Elizabeth Phillips

Publisher: Elizabeth Phillips

HEREFORD
The Late Tudor and Early Stuart City and its People
0 954 85780 1

Published in September 2004 by Elizabeth Phillips

Set in 12pt Humanist by Techdoc Documentation Ltd.
Produced and Printed by Jasprint Digital
and Antony Rowe Ltd.

Acknowledgements

My greatest debt is to the late Penelope Morgan without whose monumental transcription of the City records I could not have attempted this study. She has made these records accessible to any one who cares to take them from the Record Office shelves. I must also thank Anthea Brian who introduced me to the Record Office and the Cathedral library and has helped with criticism and guidance. I am indebted as well to Ann Cosway, Rosalind Caird and Sue Hubbard who have read this through and corrected some of my mistakes and to Sue in particular for helping with Latin translation.

I would also like to thank All Saints Church, Hereford Library, Herefordshire Record Office, Hereford Museum and Fotomas Index for permission to use their pictures. The staff of the Record Office and the Cathedral Library have been unfailingly kind and helpful.

Last of all I thank my husband for reading this through several times, correcting my spelling and punctuation and encouraging me to persevere despite having to put up with me peering at my computer evening after evening.

Table of Contents

Introduction

History is not just about wars, dates, great events and the affairs of monarchs and national leaders. As important and more interesting is how ordinary people carried on their lives while these events were going on. During the late sixteenth and early seventeenth centuries England went through turbulent times but from their records it seems that Herefordians were able to lead their lives relatively unaffected.

Hereford has a very good collection of records dating from this period. There are two printed sources, Speed's map of 1610 and Leland's description of his journeys through Hereford made between 1535 and 1538. Taylor's map of 1757 is also useful as it is very detailed and shows the city before the demolition of most of the old buildings. The Cathedral Archives give an insight into the domestic life of the cathedral and the considerable amount of property owned by its clergy in the city. The most extensive collection is in the County Record Office which holds a good series of records of the proceedings of the Mayors court, Quarter sessions and Lawdays as well as the Mayors Great Black Book which records proclamations made by the mayor lists of members of the city council and of members of the guilds. There are also various sets of accounts, parish records and other documents such as tax assessments and occasional wills, inventories and letters. In some of them the people are recorded speaking for themselves. Many of these documents were transcribed by the late Penelope Morgan and can now be found in bound volumes on the open shelves in the Record Office. Unfortunately there are records missing because in 1836 a cleaner in the old town hall, where they were stored in sheepskin sacks, sold them for scrap paper. Luckily, the town clerk was able to rescue a great part of them.

The Record Office has a seventeenth century copy of the Custom Book. From a very early period a code of laws governing the City had been built up. When Henry the Second granted the men of Ruthlan their town in fee farm by the same customs as the men of Hereford had, the Custom Book was made as a record for Hereford and Ruthlan, 35 years before Richard I sold the City to its citizens for forty pounds. Since then it has been carefully preserved and brought forward as evidence on many important occasions. An English translation from the original Latin was made in 1486. Hereford's series of royal charters can be seen, by appointment, at the Townhall. There are no pictures from this time, the ones used here are from a later period but made before the demolition of many of the old house and the city gates.

Many papers have been written in the Transactions of the Woolhope Naturalists Field Club (T.W.N.F.C) on different topics using some of these records This paper attempts to give a rounded picture of the city and its people, using a wider selection of them. For the Latin scholar there is a wealth of further information in both the Cathedral archives and the Record office. These are only the records actually in the city there are others in archives across the country.

As well as the written evidence the city itself is a record of its history. The street plan within the walls, parts of which still stand, is virtually the same as that shown by Speed's map so it is very easy to imagine the city as it was 400 years ago.

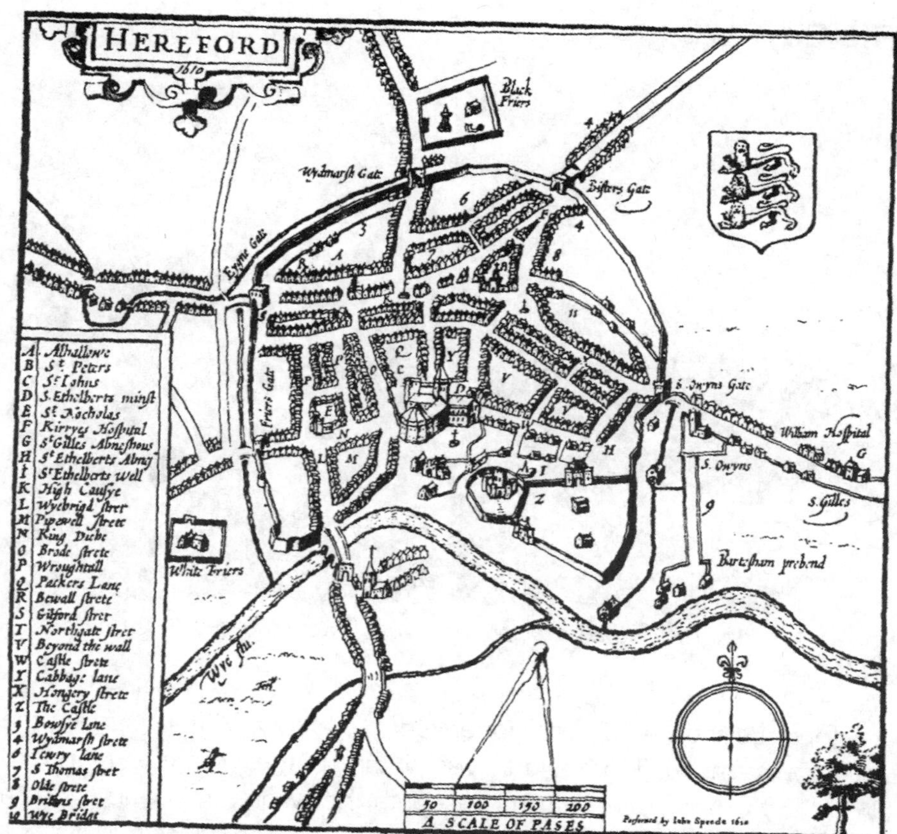

Speed's Map 1610

The City

The Cathedral before the West Tower collapsed

John Leland, who was appointed by Henry VIII to survey the antiquities of his kingdom and to visit all the libraries, came to Hereford about 1535. Approaching from the south; he wrote, 'my journey from Monmouth to Hereford brought me over a large stone bridge built on four arches. Hereford is a large old town with strong walls and a mighty castle next to the bank of the river Wye. I estimate that the circumference of this castle is as great as that of Windsor. Its keep is tall and strong, and in the ditch close to the keep is a good spring called St Ethelbert's Well. Hereford town wall is surrounded by a ditch which is always full of stagnant water. This drains down and collects in the ditch, where it is retained by some mills which are driven by it before it flows into the valley of the Wye. Were it not for the mills the ditch would often be dry. The town has four parish churches including one in the cathedral (St John's). The suburbs of Hereford contain two parish churches, a Benedictine priory dependent on Gloucester Abbey, and two friaries, black and grey.' At about the time that Leland wrote, the two friaries were dissolved and four of the mills, two for corn and two fulling mills belonging to the Dean and Chapter were destroyed by order of Henry VIII. The reason for this is not clear but possibly it was because the local clergy opposed the changes he was making in the Church. Great distress was caused in the city and its woollen industry was destroyed. Despite later efforts to revive it, it never recovered. After saying how big the castle was, Leland goes on to say that it was verging on ruin and the bridge over the ditch (South of Castle Street) had completely collapsed. On the other hand, he says the city walls were maintained in excellent condition by the Hereford burgesses. Speed's map shows they were still there with their six gates in 1610. Each of these gates had a porter appointed by the council. Among other duties, they had to open the gates at daybreak, lock them at 10 p.m. and give surety of £40 for their safekeeping. For this there was no regular salary and in 1576 they complained that although when Richard Phillips was mayor they had been paid, they 'now get no recompense or wages nor any other commodity for their pains', even though they often had to get out of their beds to let people in.[1]

Not everyone treated the wall with respect. In 1555 John Hampton, a painter, was sent to prison for seven days because, 'he broke and perished a piece of the city wall in Bowsey lane and took thirty-four stones from it to the great decaying of the same and a bad example to other evil disposed persons'.[2]

By 1618 it seems not to have been so well-maintained because Edward Perkins and Mary, his mother, complained that they rented land at Saint Owen's gate and the town wall had fallen and made the ground useless. Their claim for a remedy was referred to the common council.3[3]

Although the gates were so well guarded, in 1579 Thomas Church, a dyer, was allowed to make a little door through the wall from his workshop near Widemarsh Gate so he could wash his cloth in the (stagnant) town ditch. It may be significant that he was a councillor and became mayor in 1586. The Farmers Club at the end of Widemarsh Street is the only part of a gate still standing. Thomas Church 's door can still be seen from the ring road.

St Owen's Church which stood outside Saint Owens Gate was demolished during the civil war as it was a defence risk. Hungrie Street led out through the gate to St Giles almshouse which according to Leland was presented to the city by King Richard II in 1299 haviing previously been a chapel belonging to the Franciscans and the Templars. The mayor elected the chaplain and one of the aldermen was the custos and did the accounts. A petition of 1567, said St Giles had always had a resident chaplain but 'one had crept in' who did not reside with them, leaving the house, orchard and garden worth £20 per annum empty and he received five marks* (mark = 13s 4d) per annum. The petitioners wanted the parson of St Owen's to be chaplain and the house and garden divided between two more poor men. The beadsmen 'were not to beg or be common haunters of ale houses and to be daily drunk as they are presently.' The petition was not granted; the chaplain was to stay and do his duty.[4]

The Cathedral at this time had a tower on the west front and a spire on the central tower. The spire was removed when the west front was restored after collapsing in 1786. Saint Martins church, blown up in the civil war, was south of Wye Bridge behind the Saracen's Head. Saint Nicholas was in the middle of King Street where it widens by the Orange Tree Pub.

The last of the six gates was at the south end of Wye Bridge. As the only river crossing the bridge was vital, but, in 1596 the inhabitants of Wyebridge ward petitioned the council

`Wyebridge is altogether ruinous and fallen into decay'.[5] They wanted five shillings per annum out of every ward of the city for six years and the annuities of the city towards the repair of the bridge and to choose yearly two or three honest and substantial citizens to see the money bestowed accordingly. This was agreed.

The record of the examination of Thomas Hycken, charged with affray with Master Harvard 's servant, gives an interesting picture of life in the town. Hycken was a thirty-year-old sawyer who lived in Woolhope. He said he came up to Hereford to work, staying one night at Mordiford. The first day he bought shoes at a shoemakers house near All Saints church then went straight back to William Cookes house outside St Owens gate, there bought a two penny loaf and beans and went back to Woolhope till Tuesday night when he stayed in Sculls house in Mordiford. By five o'clock on Wednesday morning, he was at the house of Thomas Boyle and went sawing outside Friern (Friars) gate till seven in the evening. Then he went to John Taylor's and sat down and drank 'in company of two tylers, a little fellow, a tailor and the goodwife of the house for half an hour, then to bed'. Next day, he worked from five in the morning till seven in the evening when he went to Thomas Boyle's house to supper until 8 o'clock. Then he went 'to Taylor's house and ` stood a while in the door and then came in a woman at Widemarsh gate with a pail of clothes on her head, being a maid servant to Johan Washers'. After she had gone he went back into the house for about a quarter of an hour. 'As he came out by the door, he saw the same woman coming back and demanded of her where she had been with her clothes. She answered she had brought the clothes to the place whereunto she was appointed to bring them'. So he went further at Widemarsh gate with her and ` so down by the town ditch side to Bysters gate. One of the prisoners there said "farewell Thomas Hycken" and he said "God be with thee Cooper and God help thee" and so down by the town ditchside until they came to the rails there, then he left the maid and went to the house of William Cooke and his wife and met one Tynker and drank with them about an hour.'[6]

Two important buildings are not on the 1610 map but are shown on Taylor's map of 1757. The Tolsey stood at the entrance to Commercial Street from High Town in the middle of the road. At different times, it was a meeting place for the trade guilds and the Council. By the end of the 16th century, it was used for storing records and the city treasure chest and some of the city's weapons. The other missing building is the Market Hall, probably built in 1576 by John Abel, the master carpenter. This was in High Town; it was demolished in 1862, and the site is now marked with black bricks for each of its supporting columns. The open space beneath was where fruit and vegetables were sold. The middle floor was a meeting hall for city and county business. On the top floor were fourteen chambers, one for each of the city trade guilds. It was said to be the biggest market hall in the country. To build such a hall required a certain level of prosperity but there is no evidence of how it was financed. Even the date of building is uncertain. When it was demolished in 1862 a beam was found with the date 1576 on it. Although it could have come from an earlier structure it is unlikely that second-hand timber would have been used in what was a prestige building.

Where the Old House stands there was a row of houses where the butchers had their shops, behind them was Cooken Row where the bakers lived and worked.

Cooken Row James Wathen 1797

At least one of the houses in this area, next to St Peter's, was of high status as an inventory taken when it was leased with its contents in 1567 shows:

In the great chamber: the hangings of new work and a cupboard
In the chimney chamber: a bedstead with girths* 1 coffer and the hangings
*Girths – webbing to support the mattress.
In the middle chamber: a bedstead with a tester to the same, a great coffer with 2 locks, a new press and the hangings.
In the stair chamber: a bedstead with cords (to support the mattress) a coffer and the hangings.
In the chamber by the court: a great chest with 3 locks and covered with leather, a table of wainscot, 2 stools and the hangings.
In the hall: a large table with 2 forms of wainscot the trestles and the 'sylinge' of wainscot, the hangings and a cupboard with 2 locks.

In the great parlour: a great table with his frames all of wainscot and the wainscot round about the same place.
In the little parlour: a table with the frames and 2 forms, one large cupboard with 3 locks, all of wainscot and the wainscot and hangings about the same.
In the buttery: a cupboard and 3 shelves.
In the great kitchen: a new furnace of brass and the shelves round about the same.
In the little kitchen: a great trow with a cover, the dresser and the shelves about.
In the larder house: a table with trestles and shelves round about and a sieve covered with hair.
In the chamber over the larder house: 2 standing beds with boards, a coffer, a counter table.
In the bolting house a great cubbe [cupboard] 3 trows and a bolting tub.
Item the glass and lattice of the whole house.[7]

Not all the city's houses were as grand as this one; many would have been more like the one that Bartholomew Edwards was supposed to build on a garden in Saint Owen's as a condition of his lease from the Vicars Choral, 'He shall build upon the garden a tenement of two rooms well lofted with a double chimney in the midst.' [8]

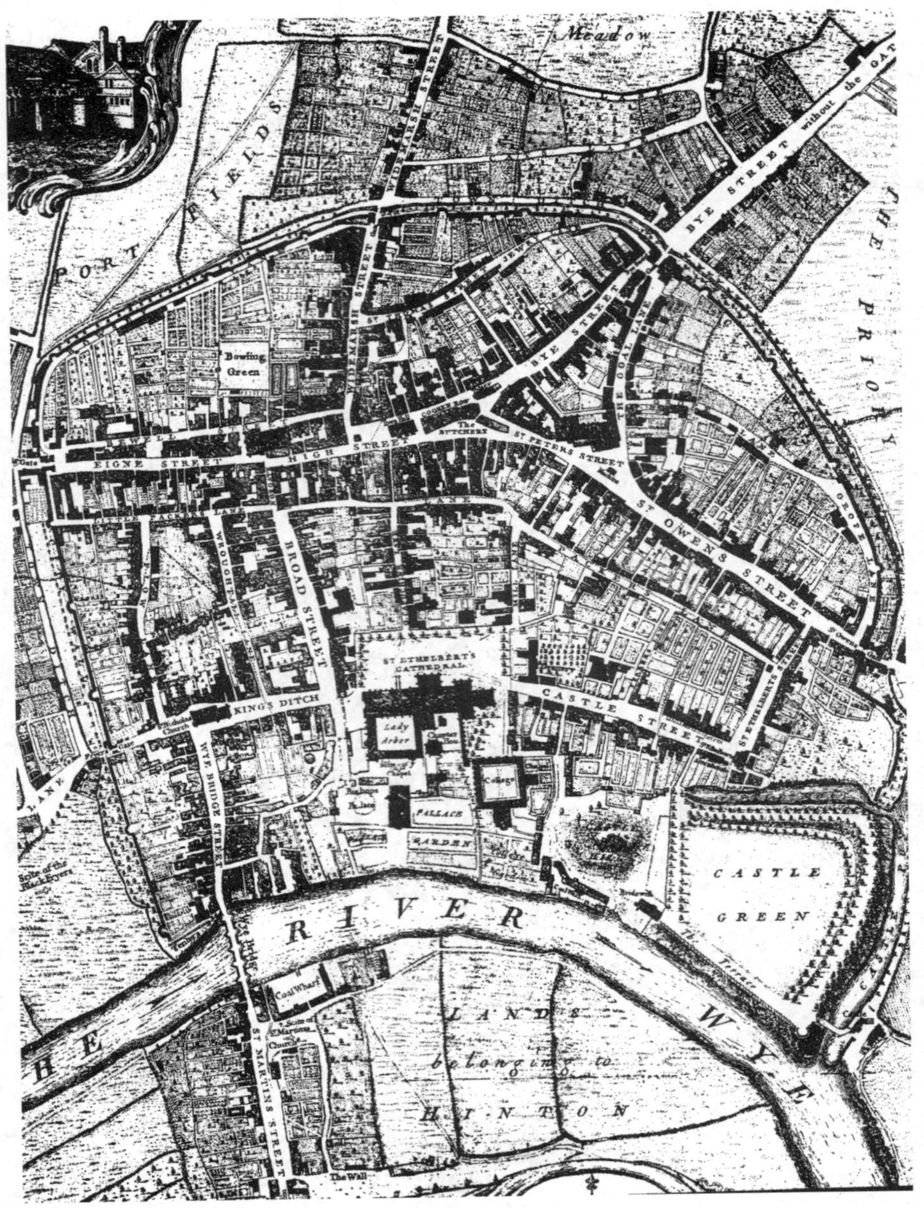

Taylors map 1757

Widemarsh

Widemarsh Gate James Wathen 1798

Widemarsh Common was a great asset to the city. According to the Custom Book, Richard I granted the city eight townships to replace those granted to the Cathedral by previous kings. One of them was Wigmarsh Moor.

Duncombe[9] says that the suburb of Widemarsh was joined on the North by a tract of wasteland called Widemarsh, which was partly enclosed in 1541. In 1542, this parcel was leased to Richard Welsh for twelve years. The 150 acres of waste remaining was situated in the parishes of Holmer, St John's, and St Peter's.

The ownership of a parcel of land called New Widemarsh must have been in dispute between the parish of Holmer, which adjoins it on the north, and the City. At a cause heard by the Council of the Marches meeting in Hereford in 1552 it was decided that from February 1st to August 1st the Mayor and citizens of Hereford should have the feeding and pasturage uninterrupted and the tenants and inhabitants of Holmer, Over Shelwick, Nether Shelwick, Wigmarsh Moor and Kentish Burcott should have it from August 1st to the end of November. From December 1st to January 31st, the use was common to both parties.[10] All the land adjoining the marsh had to be fenced off from it.

Fifteen days before the Council of the Marches (see P.22) visited Hereford the marsh was to be cleared and devoted to their horses and geldings. Four persons were to guard them day and night and the Council was to pay a penny per night over the watchmen's charges. The accounts for 1554/55 for Eigne, Widemarsh, Bisters and St Owens wards have entries for the cost of breakfast and drinks for the keepers during the "driving of Widemarsh" and payments of 8d a day and a night for the keeping of Widemarsh for from ten to thirteen days. Widemarsh and St Owens paid a penny to the bellman; perhaps he proclaimed the driving so that owners could collect their animals. Hereford and Holmer held a further parcel of land called Old Widemarsh 'jointly and promiscuously'. Hereford also held Monkmoor, about fifteen acres.

The availability of this large area of pasture was invaluable to the city. There are no complete records for any one year but the ones we have show about eighty horses and cows being put out by three of the five wards so probably about a hundred animals, mostly horses would be out there. There would have been difficulty accommodating and feeding this number within the City. The charges for these animals, a half-crown per annum for a horse and two shillings for a cow, provided funds for paving the streets and repairing bridges and pumps. Pigs appear to have been put on the marsh free but an order of 1625 said that `Swine put on the pasture called Widemarshe and Munckemoore are to be yoked and ringed before May 20th and kept yoked until the end of harvest and ringed yearly from tyme to tyme uppon payne of 5s 8d.'[11]

Each of the five city wards appointed two keepers of Widemarsh every year. They kept an account of the beasts put on the marsh, putting a mark, probably for the ward, with hot pitch on each one. The accounts have regular entries for 'pitch, tallow, and coles'. These accounts, showing the owner of each animal, had to be presented every year at Michaelmas. As a scribe was employed to write them it would be interesting to know how the keepers kept their records and whether the animals had all to be put out on a given day and paid for then; in some years there are entries for money owing for tack. As the horses would have been for working or riding they could presumably have been taken back and forth once they were marked. As well as checking the animals, the keepers were responsible for 'tending' the marsh. Their accounts show payments for enclosing, ditching, trenching, 'shereing of the wont [mole] hillocks' and to Goodman Glade for killing the moles, half-a-crown. They also paid for mending the gate and, almost annually, locks and keys. The balance of the money collected was used for the upkeep of the city, the mayor issuing warrants authorising the keepers to pay for various projects.

Considerable areas of the city were paved with Widemarsh money. For instance, in 1596, one ward, unnamed, paid Nicholas Bayley for paving fifty yards near St Peter's, eighty-eight yards behind the Boothall and fifty yards at the Milk Lane (St John Street) End: he was paid 1 ½ pence a yard. Stone at eightpence a load, gravel at fourpence and sand at fourpence were supplied by Roger Eysham. In the same year, the keepers for Widemarsh ward were authorised to pay twenty-five shillings (equal to 200 yards) to the paviors for paving its streets. Brian Newton, the mayor, instructed Widemarsh ward to lend Saint Owen's six shillings and eight pence for paving in Packers Lane (East St). In 1608 repairs costing twenty eight shillings and sevenpence were made to St Thomas Street.

Widemarsh money contributed towards the upkeep of the city's water supplies. In 1554/5 there is a detailed account of making a 'plompe'. In 1603 Walter Hurdman ordered Eigne ward to pay fifteen shillings to Barnabe Smyth for 'reedifying' the pump in the High Street near All Saints church and in 1608 eleven shillings was 'bestowed upon paving and repairing and setting up the stones in the defence of a house adjoining the pump in Widemarsh ward'.[12] Three table stones, a bar of iron and three rails were also provided so it sounds as if people waiting for water were either careless or rowdy! The well at the 'toulsinge end' (Tolsey end) was cleaned and a new bucket and chain provided at a cost of 10s 8d and eight shillings was paid for mending the 'lour well and for the chain' in 1608.

In 1596, when the inhabitants of Wyebridge ward complained about the condition of Wyebridge their Widemarsh keepers had to pay 14s 2d toward repairing Wyebridge 'being in decay'. As well as paying toward the fabric of the city, Widemarsh money paid part of the wages of the clerk of St Peters for ringing the common bell and of the two beadles. An interesting entry shows a payment made in 1625 to Thomas Curthose from 'the tacke of Widemarsh to be employed for and toward the building of the House of Correction'.[13] The building of houses of correction or Bridewells with stocks of material to set the idle to work was authorised nationally in 1576.

There was possibly another dispute over ownership of the marsh in 1618 as in that year Richard Gravel met Richard Weaver and Richard Bullock, Councillors, in Broad Street and taunted them `are you angry because we have recovered Widemarsh from you?'[14] Unfortunately, there is no information about the identity of 'we'.

A hint that the marsh may have seen some disreputable goings on comes in the case brought by James Barroll, chief constable, who, in the course of his duties was abused by Thomas Luggard, his wife and son. The son's contribution to a rich torrent of insults was 'goe to Widemarsh and take up the wenches clothes and blow tobacco in her tayle'.[15]

Another misuse of this open space was for the disposal of waste. At a lawday in 1576 it was agreed 'that where divers persons do make dunghills and lay great heaps of dung as well within the common of Widemarsh as to sundry other places, not allowed for common mixens (rubbish heaps), within streets lanes and highways within the liberties of the city, to the great annoyance of Her Majesties liege people and sclaunder of the city. At all times after this ordinance openly proclaimed to all and every person to take and carry away the said heaps and dunghills without any contradiction of any person. And moreover, the bellman having with him the town clerk's man shall within eight days here following openly proclaim and publish the ordinances above recited in every ward so everyone it touches may take notice and thereupon the same to take effect.'[16]

Widemarsh was enclosed in 1774 by act of Parliament. The commissioners appointed, all local dignitaries, allotted the residue of the waste, after they had dealt with the claims of all other interested parties, to pay for' lighting, paving, pitching and repairing the streets lanes and passages of Hereford and its suburbs' very much as it had been doing. They were also careful to see that a series of narrow enclosures in the form of a circle should be left as a racecourse. Even today, the rump of Widemarsh provides the city with a space for games.[17]

Some examples of the keepers accounts:

1600

The keepers desire allowance as followeth
To the keeper in money 5s 4d
To the beddles in money 3s 4d
Toward the lock and for pyche 6d
A hoke to hang the chaines at inge gatt in money 12d
To Walter Bodnam for ringing the common bell 12d
The caridge of 19 lodd of gravell within inge gatt in money 6s 4d
Three lodd of stone 2s.
For paving within Inge Gatt in money 14s 11d
(i.e. 119 yards)
For makinge of a cassey from Parise Barn unto the Sickment Cassey being 32 yardes 4s
Cariege of 7 lod of ston at 8d the lod 4s 8d
Payed more for the cariege of 6 lod of gravell at 4d the lod 2s
More for the cariege of 5 lod of stone 3s 4d
More for the cariege of 4 lod of gravell 16d
For the paving of the cassey by the Sickment 8s 9d (65 yards)
Cariege of 2 lod of stone 16d
Cariege of 8 lod of gravell 2s 8d
For paving by the sickment 40 yards 5s
Cariege of rubble 4d
2 lods of stone more within Inge Gatt 16d
Making this accompte 6d
Whole some layd out is £3 9 8

Remayneth 4s 6d[18]

1596 Keepers George Beynam and Morgan Aprice desire to be allowed as foloweth viz.
Paid for tydinge and ditchinge 2s 8d
Paid to the keeper for his wages 2s 8d
Paid to the clarke of St Peeters for ringinge the comen bell 7d.
Paid by the comaundement of Mr Bryan Newton gent late mayor of this cittie to Nicholas Bayley for pavinge behinde the bowthe hall in the said cittie 12s
Paid to the said Nicholas Bayly for paving 55 yards neere St Peeters crosse 7s
Paid for 8 lodes of sand to Roger Eysham att 4d the lode 2s 8d
Paid to Roger Eysham for a lode of stone and a lode of sande 12d
Paid to Eysham for 2 lodes of stone att 8d the lode 16d
Paid for a locke key pitch tallow and coles 6d
Paid to Eysham for one lode of stone and another of sand 12d
Paid to the said Nicholas Bayly for paving 50 yards att the Milke Lane end 6s
Paid to the clerke for writinge this accompte 6d
Summa 38s 4d[19]

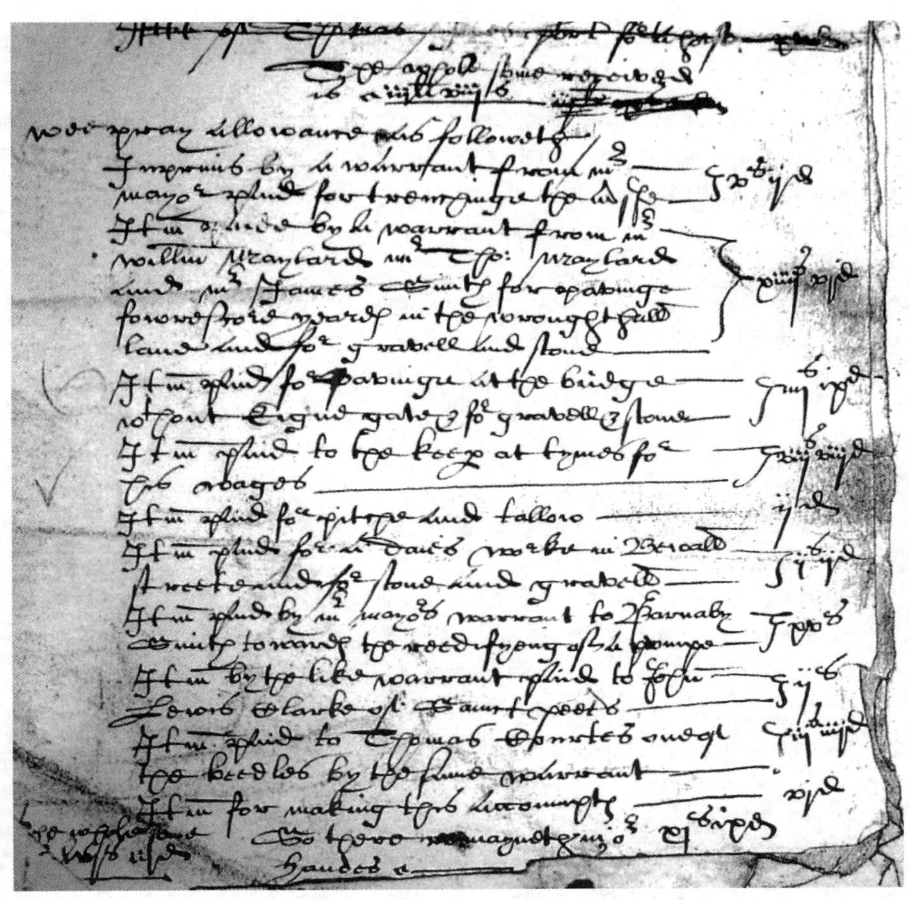

A page from the Keepers accounts

The Common Council

As well as duties similar to those carried out by the City Council today: street cleaning, lighting, control of local markets and rubbish disposal, the 16th century common council or 'Election' was responsible for maintaining law and order and enforcing not just their own regulations but national statutes and proclamations as well .

The mayor, who held office for a year, and the six aldermen, who were elected for life, all became JPs. They had the town clerk to advise them on points of law, four Sergeants at Mace to carry out summonses and make arrests and two unpaid constables in each ward. There were two beadles who had to watch for beggars and vagrants, visit every house monthly to warn them against keeping swine or ducks in the street and impound any found wandering in the city and any un-ringed swine on Widemarsh Common. For this, they got 13s 4d per annum and a gown with the city badge on the left shoulder. On market days, they controlled traffic. There was also a ceremonial sword bearer paid two pounds per annum and two chamberlains who collected rents on property owned by the council and acted as treasurers. The mayor received £10 per annum but often spent more. However the office was to be respected and anyone who insulted the mayor could end up in jail as did William Cooper who, among other insults, said that 'Master Mayor by gods wounds, was a knave and all mayors for the last twenty years past were cuckolds.' When he was brought up before the mayor and the justices `he swore forty oathes at least'[20] so had to give sureties to appear at the next sessions and in the meantime to be of good behaviour.

The bellman, who was among other things, the town crier, had to pave 200 yards of street per annum with gravel and stone provided by the chamberlains. As the charge for paving was 1½ d per yard, the question is what rewards did this post bring which made a payment of twenty five shillings worth while. The accounts of the keepers of Widemarsh show two payments of 1d to the bellman, possibly to announce 'the driving', and the accounts of St Nicholas show that the churchwardens paid 4d for a proclamation in 1601. From 1565 the bellman and the beadles were paid 2d for every swine found wandering the streets. He also had `to clense and carry away the muck dung and fylth wekely happening or left in the high Causey and in the market place within Broad Street'. For this he was to receive twenty shillings per annum being over and above the twenty shillings already allowed to him.[21] When few people could read it was not enough to fix government proclamations and local regulations to a post in the market place, they had to be proclaimed by the bellman accompanied by the town clerk's man. Presumably his twenty shilling wage covered this duty but possibly he could earn extra for other announcements such as what appears to be this private proclamation of Saturday, 8th April 1605, 'Be it known that Margaret Parry, wife of John Parry of Aconbury has left him, not only to her said husbands disgrace but to the great hurt and undoing of him in selling, wasting and consuming of his substance and goods. Anyone who deals with her does so at their own risk.' [22]

Bisters Gate James Wathen 1795

There were two prisons, in Bysters Gate for people with no money or influence and in the Boothall for anyone who could provide surety, or was a freeman. Boothall prisoners could go to church at Saint Peters with a keeper or out to dine with friends or learned counsel.

Included with the property handed from mayor to mayor were, 'five pairs of bolts (for fastening the legs), five pairs of gyves (fetters), two pairs of arm bolts, one neck collar',[23] so imprisonment could be harsh. A coroners list for 1625 shows that six people died in prison of `God's visitation'.

Each of the five wards was supposed to have a pair of stocks. For 1625 there is `a note of what James Barrall have laid out by the commandment of Mr Meyers:

Item paid for timber for the stokes	5s 6d
Item paid for eyernes (irons) the some of	5s 2d
Item dd in nailes for the some	10d
Paid for mackeing	18d
1 horce lock and key	16d[24]

The mayors court could not deal with serious felonies, in these cases the prisoners had to be handed over to the sheriff for trial at the Assizes.

Justice was administered by several courts whose origins go back to the distant past so it is difficult to discover how they all functioned, but, from the evidence of the records, by the sixteenth century,the Mayors Court,which dealt with cases of debt and trespass, the Tourn, the Quarter Sessions and the two Lawdays were the main instruments for the administration and control of the city. The Lawdays seem to have originated from the two inquisitions, the first of which, according to 'The Customs Book' was the general inquisition which was held outside the gates of the city between the Feasts of St Michael and All Saints. All the citizens of the liberties of the city had to attend 'and present all such things as concern the state of the city and view of frankpledge'. The second inquisition majus general was to be called by the mayor in the most public place in the city. All the 'discreetest' of the city were warned to attend. At each lawday, three inquests were elected; the first from among the thirty three members of the council (the election) the second from the most substantial citizens dwelling within the city walls and the third from those from outside the walls although by this time this order was no longer strictly adhered to.[23] They were obliged under pain of a fine to attend the lawdays to discuss new regulations and give judgement on the various complaints, petitions and accusations brought before the mayor and his brethren (the aldermen). The Tourn was originally when the sheriff toured the shire twice yearly and visited each hundred court and acted as judge. Serious cases were dealt with by the Assize Courts. People arrested by the constables were brought before the mayor for examination; their words were recorded by clerks, often as they were spoken. The first inquest was the most powerful and could veto decisions of the other two. Only freemen could vote for the council, the Mayor being chosen from among them, by them. This led to control of the city ending in the hands of a small group of families; the names Church, Hurdman, Price, Boyle, Warnecombe, Carwardine and Maylard are among those which crop up serving as mayors, MPs and masters of the powerful guilds merchant year after year. Even so, some of them, when they were not the serving mayor, were presented before him for wrong-doing. Such was the case of Gregory Price, mayor in 1577 and Sheriff of the County in 1566 when the mayor proclaimed 'Gregory Prise Esq., hath this present yere wrongfully enclosed to hymselfe severall the Priory Portfields which tyme out of mind of man hath yerely after the rake byn common to the citizens of the seid citie and turned the water curse of Monkmore (which curse also tyme out of mind of man hath at all tymes of the yere byn common to the said citizens) to the losse of the common pasture thereof and to the losse and hynderans of the citezens and in habitants of the said city and also hathe caused the auncient stanke at Inegate whyche conveyed the waters thereof to the grene towndyche and the longe towndyche to be broken and destried in the nyght tyme. And over that dydde mynster oncitting words as well to the chamberlains of the said citie on doyng there offices for the redresse thereof'.[25]

The composition of the Council, the right of the mayor and aldermen to be Justices of the Peace, the privileges of the citizens and the guilds merchant, the right to hold fairs and markets and collect the tolls were granted by a series of charters. The first of these was granted by Richard I in 1189 when he granted the citizens the right to hold the city in perpetuity for a rent of £40 and made them responsible for maintaining the city defences. In the great charter of 1597 Elizabeth I confirmed all the previous charters and granted the city corporate status. In 1973 Elizabeth II ratified Hereford's status as a city.

The Council of the Marches

Because it was in one of the marcher counties Hereford came under the jurisdiction of the Council of the Marches. This body, based at Ludlow, had been given its final form by Henry VIII. Its purpose was originally to control the Welsh and the Marcher Lords, but in 1536 royal law was brought directly into Wales, so, by Elizabeth's reign, Wales was thought to have been 'brought from their disobedient, barbarous and (as may be termed) lawless incivility to the civil and obedient estate they now remain'.[26] The Council was headed by a president - for a time during this period, Sir Henry Sidney, father of the more famous Philip, held the post. Some government communications were sent to the Council of the Marches to be passed on to county and city JPs, others went straight to the mayor. For Hereford, the Council of the Marches acted to keep control of the mayor and his brethren, making sure there was no partial dealing, acting as a court of appeal for citizens who felt they had been unfairly dealt with and adjudicating in disputes such as the one over Widemarsh, where the council were involved. In 1565 there was a complaint to John Scudamore, one of the Queen's Council of the Marches, that 'the ffryse men & Welsh clothiers are being molested so that they sell their wares outside the liberties to the hindrance of the said city and specyally of the ffermor of the Boothhall.' Though he had been told, the mayor had done nothing.[27]

The Council of the Marches could deal with cases of treason and other serious felonies. In 1585 the mayor was ordered to search out five men accused by John Price of being rebels and send them to the Council.

The President and Council visited Hereford periodically causing major disruption when they did. In 1557, as well as taking over Widemarsh for their horses, leading citizens were told what they had to provide; every thing from a bed in their house or a stable for eight horses to towels, napkins, and a gridiron.

In order to provide food for this influx, traders from outside the city, usually strictly controlled, were to be allowed to come into the city. In February 1588 an order came from the Council of the Marches to the mayor 'that whereas none are suffered to sell within the city any flesh killed or bread baked out of the city, which may breed great scarcity there during the time the president and council make their abode there, by reason of the great assembly of people resorting to the council, he shall therefore make proclamation that it shall be lawful during that time for all persons of what country or place whatever, to resort thither on Wednesday and Saturday with any kind of wholesome victuals as flesh, fish, bread, and candles with hide and tallow therewith, to be sold free of molestation.'

With obscure logic some citizens took advantage of this relaxation to eat meat in Lent and were duly rebuked; 'where as by some evil and lewd persons the preceding order has been misconstrued and speeches given out that liberty was given to the citizens and others to eat flesh in lent time which was not the meaning of the council but that Lent and all other days prohibited from flesh should be strictly kept.' The mayor was to proclaim that, ' all persons found faulty shall be sent for to answer the same'.[28]

Control of the People

With no police force or standing army, central government was very concerned that the common people, 'the many headed monster' might get out of control. Ket's rebellion in Norfolk against enclosure and the Pilgrimage of Grace against religious change had been led by common men. The availability of printed material in English was regarded with suspicion as it could propagte subversive ideas. Numbers (probably exaggerated) of 'masterless men' and discharged soldiers roaming the countryside caused the ruling classes great alarm. A contemporary summed up their fears 'the multitude are always dangerous to the peace of the kingdom and having nothing to lose willingly embrace all means of innovation in the hope of gaining something by other men's ruin'.[29]

The instinct of the governing classes was to tighten control, so the Privy Council, working through the JPs, bombarded the localities with proclamations urging them to seek out anyone perceived likely to cause trouble. In 1571, instructions came from the Queen that the constables and between two and four substantial parishioners in each parish were to search out all `rogues, vagabonds and sturdie beggars, masterless men and all persons otherwise suspected, to be punished by stocking and sharp and severe whipping according to law.'[30] They were then to be passed from constable to constable to their place of birth or last abode within three years. Similar instructions were issued periodically throughout the country.

Any stranger who could give no reason for being in the city was questioned very closely particularly if they were labourers with no obvious employment and servants who were not with their masters. Discharged soldiers were given a passport by their commanding officer when they were discharged so they could find their way home without being arrested.

Even strangers who considered themselves to be gentlemen could be taken before the mayor. Willliam Holland a gentleman from Denbigh was given a very thorough examination. He was not very co-operatve. Asked when he left Denbigh he said he did not remember, he would not answer about when he was in London and said he was in Worcester on the way to London. He was equally unhelpful about the goods he had brought with him and the material and making of his jerkin and where he had left his wife.

Finally when questioned about his horse and its equipment he obviously lost patience for, after saying he paid thirty-three shillings and four pence for his horse and fifteen shilllings for the bridle and pattrell he told the mayor `to goe looke' if he wante to know what he paid for the rest of his harness. He then refused to sign the account of his examination.[31]

Inns and ale houses were regarded as places where trouble might arise so efforts were made to reduce their number and control any activities, like card playing, that went on there. In 1609, the council was rebuked by the Privy Council because they had said there were only nine licences for keeping alehouses in the county and few or none in the city. The Privy Council thought it very strange as they knew `there be a great number within your city that do keep victualling houses without licences and you have neither suppressed nor punished them according to the form of the statute.' The mayor was to summon the constables and make them present 'all the keepers of such victualling or ale houses within your city and punish them. Be very careful and diligent as we demand an exact account'.[32] In fact, the mayor had tried, a note of 1605 exists giving the names of eighteen alehouse keepers and, in the same year, forty-four people were presented for selling ale without a licence.[33]

In 1613, the Justices of Assize within Herefordshire by direction of the Kings Majesty told the mayor and city J.P.s that they were not to allow more than thirty alehouses and ten inns and 'less if there may be' within the city limits. Sureties were to be taken for good behaviour and a copy of articles 'now in the custodie of the clerk of the peace' were to be given to every one licensed and recognizances taken. Anyone presuming to keep an ale house without a licence was to be suppressed and proceeded against. If the mayor and justices failed to do this then the Justices of Assize were to be informed. A register book was to be kept by the town clerk of all licensed houses. No brewer was to sell or deliver any beer or ale to anyone not having a licence unless for use in their own household. Brewers were to get a note of licence-holders from the town clerk. They were to sell at a price which would enable the retailer to sell at a penny quart.[34]

This apparently well- organised effort at regulation seems to have been of no avail because in 1629, ninety-two persons were listed as brewers or retail sellers of ale, many in a very small way, in the five city wards. The evidence is that the city was very well supplied with ale sellers and ale houses. Some of them, like the Starre, were disorderly: William Baker the landlord was 'suppressed from selling of ale for keeping in his house one Margery Baldwyne a comon hoore being before that tyme comaunded to putt her away and for suffering disorderly persons to drinck in his house at unreasonable hours'. In the same presentation, William Butler, who was a councillor, was committed to 'send sufficient sureties to appear the next sessions being found in an ale house at an unreasonable hour viz at 12 o'clock at midnight in the company of lewd and disordered persons'.[35]

As well as keeping ale houses in order the council appointed aletasters to test the quality of the ale. In 1619 John Prees, corvisor, (leather worker) was presented at a view of frankpledge 'being a brewer has refused to let the aletaster to taste his ale to see if it is wholesome for the body of man'.[36] An additional regulation to be enforced was to prevent the selling dressing or consuming of meat in inns during Lent. Phillip Trehearne an innkeeper, brewer, member of the council and mayor in 1622, seems to have been suspect, for in 1618 he, Richard Pleody yeoman and Roger Wellington yeoman each gave a recognisance of £30 that 'if the above bounden Phillip Trehearne innkeeper doe not dresse any fleshe in his house nor suffer any fleshe to be eaten in his house this Lent time for any respect whatsoever nor shall dresse any fleshe in his house nor suffer any fleshe to be eaten in his house nor shall make any supper of fleshe uppon Friday nights for any person whatsoever either in or out of Lent nor shall then suffer any meate to be dressed or eaten in his house that then this recognizance to be void otherwise to remain in full strength and vertue.[37]

In 1620 Edward Trehearne servant to Phillip Trehearne innholder deposed that there was no flesh eaten or dressed in the house of his master this last Lent. Examined whether Mr Hablyn and or Mr Jeffries had any flesh at table in the said house or ate any he denied it.[38]

Phillip Trehearne was probably regarded as a troublemaker because he had been imprisoned in 1619[39] for revealing council secrets to outsiders and refusing to pay his assessment towards getting a renewal of the city charter and encouraging others to do the same saying `that it was but faction and of purpose to serve private men's turns'. He threatened to appeal to the Privy Council. He was presented again but still refused to yield.

After the reformation the people lost one of their entertainments and the city gained income. The Great Black Book records that in 1549 John Warnecombe, the then mayor declared that as the pageants performed on the Feast of Corpus Christi by the trade guilds and corporations had been suppressed the money spent on them should be used to pay for repairs to 'ruinous and decayed causeys, pavements, streets, walls and casting of the town dytches'.[40] No doubt the city authorities would have seen the pageants as a focus for trouble and rowdyism and possibly religious dissent among their citizens and been glad to see the end of them.

The Poor

One reason why the multitude had become a threat was that so many of them had literally nothing to lose because of acute poverty. During the sixteenth century, the population of england and wales is estimated to have risen from about three million to nearly four and a half million. As agriculture was not flexible enough to adapt to feeding the growing numbers, prices went up. There were too many workers available so wages stayed the same or went down and many of the unemployed joined the ranks of sturdy beggars. At the beginning of the century, the authorities made little distinction between those who could work and didn't choose to and those who wanted to work but could not. They were all given the same harsh treatment. The problem was made worse by the dissolution of the monasteries which had previously cared for the poor, so provision for them fell increasingly on the local authorities and private charity. In Hereford in 1550, a survey was carried out of all those with stores of grain, so that it could be used to relieve the poor. The lists exist for Wyebridge, Saint Owen's, and Eigne wards.

It seems that here was an early recognition that not all the poor were wilfully idle; the next year, seventeen people, ten of them women, were given help, some with an allowance from their parish, some to labour, two women were to be partly helped and partly to labour because they had children. In 1555, there was an appeal from the Mayor to the Queen (Mary) for help with poor relief. A list was attached of forty poor and impotent persons remaining in the city that were receiving relief and thirty eight the mayor and citizens reckoned they could not help. They wanted licences for them to beg in the County in whichever parishes the County Justices decided. Licensed begging was permitted, an indication that attitudes were beginning to soften. The population of Hereford at this time would have been around 3,500. If seventy-eight was the total number of people needing help, at two percent the level of destitution was fairly low at a time when between thirty and forty percent of the national population was thought to be on the bread-line.

During the reign of Elizabeth a series of poor laws was enacted which recognised that there was a difference between those who couldn't and those who wouldn't work. William Harrison, vicar of Radwinter in Essex, writing of his own times around 1583, described how the poor were classified. 'With us the poor is commonly divided into three sorts, so that some are poor by impotence as the fatherless child, the aged, blind and lame and the diseased person that is judged to be incurable; the second are poor by casualty, as the wounded soldier, the decayed householder, and the sick person visited with grievous and painful diseases; the third consisteth of thriftless poor as the rioter that hath consumed all, the vagabond that will abide nowhere but runneth up and down from place to place (as it were seeking work and finding none), and finally the rogue and the strumpet'.[41] The first two categories were to be helped, the third punished.

The Elizabethan poor laws progressed from a system of voluntary contributions to the act of 1601 which made them compulsory. The civil parishes were responsible for collection and the overseers for distribution. The records for St Peters have a list of those assessed for poor law contributions in 1622. Ninety-three people were assessed, eleven had not paid and £12 6 8 was raised. The overseers spent £12 7 4.[42] In 1617 those assessed refused to pay as non-payers the previous year had not been pursued. The accounts of the churchwardens of Saint Nicholas[43] for 1612 list three men who had not paid their ceasement (assessment) for the relief of the poor. The accounts for All Saints [44] show that they paid ninepence a week for twenty-four weeks for keeping a poor child in the parish. St Nicholas church wardens in 1613 gave practical help to two, or possibly three, children;

'Paid for two pairs of shoes for the two children 18d
Paid for the boys clothes 15½ d
Paid for shoes and hosen and the making of an old gown for the wench 2s.'

The total of 4s 9½d was a considerable amount of money.

As the poor were only entitled to receive relief in the parish of their birth or where they had established settlement, parish officials were anxious not to allow strangers to establish residence or for unsupported women to give birth in the parish. In 1624, William Skynner, gentleman, of Saint Owens parish, was presented for receiving John Hull, a stranger with his wife and children, who were likely to be, 'troublesome and chargeable unto the parish of St Owen's. He is either to remove them or give surety to the parish before Christmas'.[45] In the same year, William Knell, mason, was ordered to pay sixpence per week towards the 'maintenance of a man child got by him on the body of Joan Franklin either to Joan or the church wardens of St Peters and to give sureties for the performance thereof to save St Peters parish harmless from the maintenance of said child.'[46]

One of the duties of midwives was to try to find out from the unmarried mother who the was father of the child, in extreme cases by withholding help during labour. In a case of 1624 George Gollefor, tailor, accused his journeyman George Partrich of poisoning Anne Parsons a servant in the same house. Having got her pregnant Partrich tried to abort the child by giving her a drink thought to contain the herb savin. The midwife and other experienced women had 'searched the girl and she had confessed that Partrich was the father'. He disappeared until he heard the girl had died then he came back in 'glorious vaunting manner' and said if anyone had done it, it was George Gollefor. He came in 'peremptory and saucy manner to the shop door' and when Mrs. Gollefor told him to go away he said 'although she was his dame he did not care a fart for her and carried in fleering and scoffing about the shop'.[47] The result of the case is not known but George Partrich occurs in the records later so presumably it was not proved.

An example of a deserving pauper was Thomas Merick who, in 1618 pleaded to have his 6d weekly allowance paid. He had no one to help him and eight children. He had lived in the city forty years 'upon my trewe laboure' and had become unable to work because of his 'miserable lameness.' A warrant was made to the chief constable to bring the overseers before Mr. Mayor and to pay the money and add a penny weekly, still a pitifully small amount when a labourer could earn sixpence a day.[48] In 1554 John Smyth, a draper eighty years old, petitioned the mayor saying he had been a freeman for fifty years and nine years warden of the smiths occupation but had `fallen into gret necessyte and povertye, so that for lacke of abbyllytie to labor and of substaunce he is now lyke to peryshe for wante of ffode and sustenaunce'.... `May it plese yor goodnes of yor accustomed pitie to admytte yor said beadman to be one of the almes men of Saynt Gyles, there to do, receave and enioye accordingly as other almes men and this for the love of god and in the waye of charyte.'[49] The three inquests agreed.

Apart from Saint Giles, there were other almshouses. Saint Ethelberts was one of the oldest. It was set up in 1225, and the Bishops of Salisbury, Ely and Coventry and Hugh Foliot of Hereford and susequent bishop,s[50] promised indulgences to those who contributed towards the building. It originally had its Almshall in Broad Street, but moved to Castle Street in the middle of the sixteenth century. The Treasurer of the cathedral was to be custos (warden), ten ancient and poor people were to receive alms and if they wished they could dwell rent-free in houses belonging to the hospital within the city. No houses were to be let until the ten were housed as near to a church as possible. Leases were to be renewed for twenty-one years only. Each poor person was to receive a well baked loaf, free of bran, of a pound and a half after daily prayer and a penny every Saturday. If they were absent from prayers they lost their allowance for the day following.

The Lazarus or Sickmans Hospital was set up in 1600 in Above Eigne (Whitecross Rd) and consisted of six tenements for six poor widows who were selected by the parish officers of All Saints.

Kerry's Charity, Trinity Hospital, can be seen on Speed's map at the end of Bysters Street (Commercial Street). It was founded by Thomas Kerry, a London businessman who was born in Hereford. It is likely that he was one of the 15 children of John Kerry who ran the Packhorse Inn (which stood where the Kerry Arms now stands) during Mary's reign.

In his will he said that he founded it 'in duty to his father and mother and other relations for the lands and goods left him by them...also considering the infinite number of poor people, especially of the older sort, in the city of Hereford (being the place where he was born), and the small relief the same poor had.' He gave property that he owned in the city to found an almshouse for twelve poor widows and three unmarried men, one of the men to be governor. He nominated the first beneficiaries and ordered that 'there shall be a common seal to sign all business transactions with the picture of a death's head, having also this circumscription about the same viz. Memento Mori, the said common seal to be kept in a chest fast locked, in some convenient place in the hospital.' After laying down the rules for the management of the hospital he declared that if any of his own kin should apply for admission, they should be given preference. In 1600 he requested a lease on land for an addition to his almshouses. They had property in Castle Street, (East side) a messuage and garden, and a house on the North side of the garden in Bye street and a messuage called the Packhorse opposite the Hospital.

The Packhorse Inn, Kerry's hospital is on the right

Coningsby Hospital which still offers accommodation to four ex-service personnel was founded in 1614 by Sir Thomas Coningsby on the site of Blackfriars Friary, which he was granted at the Dissolution, for twelve old soldiers, mariners or serving men. Their distinctive uniform was supposed to have been copied by Nell Gwynne, a local girl, for her Hospital at Chelsea.In addition to these and other almshouses many citizens left something to the poor in their wills.

A board still in All Saints church records Wilcoxes Gift; James Wilcox gave 20 shillings rent from a house in the North Gate, a barn and garden in the Above Eigne and land in Burcot Row. He also gave 20 shillings to 'Saint Giles' without Saint Owen's'Gate' from lands left to Hugh Wilcox. By the will of Richard Lane, land was left to produce £20 per annum so that every

Saturday twelve poor persons who attended evening prayer in the cathedral received a penny loaf of good bread and sixpence in money. Several of the Vicars Choral left sums of money to give bread to the poor, often on the day of their funeral. In 1557 William Hyllar, clerk, left his bedding for the prisoners in the Bishops gaol, 'to a poor child a coat lined with blue buckram', 'twenty shillings in bread to poor people where most need is' and all his remaining goods to be sold and the money distributed among them. John Brown left three shillings to the poor of Saint John's parish, 2s 9d to the prisoners in Bysters Gate, `twenty shillings in bread to be divided among the poor on the day of my burial' and `half my (fire) woode to Margaret Wilks and the other half to be sold and the money to be divided among the poor'.[51]

Bishop Scory who died in 1585 left £200, a very large sum, to the city of Hereford to help its poorer citizens to help themselves. £100 was to be lent to two substantial clothiers to set poor folks at work and £100 was to be freely lent to twenty artificers. One of the clothiers and ten of the artificers were to live in the Bishop's fee. This well-intentioned gift eventually became lost.

In May 1618, there was a request by the leading citizens of Saint Owen's parish, to the mayor and three inquests from Richard Ravenhill Esq. alderman, Henry Maylard, gent and James Carwardine, gent, councillors, and William Foxe, clerk, parson of Saint Owens', the other petitioners also being of the same parish with the consent of the rest of the parishioners. They requested the grant of 'so much ground at the south west end of Saint Owen's church in the middle of the street there as said petitioners may build four small houses for the habitation of such poor people as they are bound by statute to relieve and they will answer for the reasonable and fit rent'. This was referred by the great inquest to the common council of the city.[52]

The accounts of St. Nicholas refer to the 'Parish house' and a payment of 15d for lime and clay to mend the poor women's houses in the lane, so it seems that they too had houses for the poor.

The Canons Bakehouse was at the Cathedral end of Castle Street. As well as baking for the Cathedral, 4,360 loaves yearly were distributed from cathedral funds. A rent roll for 1592 gives some details; 'allowed out of the

Canons Bake house for the making of the two doles for the poor people. The first dole for the poor people should be the 28th or 29th of November. The second should be the 26th January yearly:

Of rye allowed: 16 quarters 128 bushels, otherwise

Of wheat allowed: 8 quarters 64 bushels

96 bushels to a dole the whole is 192 bushels

All Saints received 400 loaves, Saint Johns 440, Saint Martins 300, Saint Nicholas 300, Saint Owens 300 and Saint Peters 300; many country parishes benefited as well.[53]

Although a more charitable attitude was being taken toward the 'deserving' poor', the government was still determined to keep control of those regarded as idle and undeserving as this proclamation shows:

'17th July 1613 from the Justices of Assize within Herefordshire by direction of the Kings Majestie. The Mayor and Justices of the Peace are to allott themselves unto all wards and lymittes of this city, the best inhabitants of every parish with the chief constable of every ward and overseers of the poor to once a month survey their parishes to see what idle and vagrant persons be there harboured and to take order for the punishments of rogues by sending them to the house of correction and also to see the poore, lame and impotente releved according to the statute, and to make a register book of all the inhabitants of every ward and to take notice of all strangers harboured and by whom and under whose rentes they are, to thende that their landlords may be dealt withall accordinge to justice for the good government and common wealth of the city and such strangers or inmates so harboured may be sent to the contrey or place of their last abode from whence they came, and the landlords punished for receiveing and harbouring them according to the law and statute' [54]

For the time and in view of the harsh treatment that could be administered to the poor, Hereford appears to have been well endowed with charitable foundations and charitably disposed citizens.

Regulation of the Market

The Market Hall; demolished 1862 reconstruction

Regulation of the market, both as a place where trade was carried on as well as the activity which went on there, was an important part of the council's duties. Their aim was to ensure the good conduct of traders and their customers and to prevent 'foreigners' i.e. people from outside the city, coming in uncontrolled to sell their goods.

There were three markets every week. Each commodity had its own area, hardware and basketware in Saint Peters Square, cattle in King Street near Saint Nicholas church, sheep in Broad Street, swine in Aubrey Street and fish at the fish boards at the back of the Booth Hall. The Market Bell was rung at 6 or 7 am, no sea coal nor corn was to be sold before then. This was to stop dealers forestalling the market - buying up all the supplies to raise prices. The Company of Smiths and Cutlers petitioned the Mayor and three inquests; - 'whereas there are certain that do forestall and regrate the sea coals coming unto this city, to the uttermost undoing of your orators. This shall be to desire your good masterships to see a redress herein taken, that no man do buy no coals in the market until such times the smiths and cutlers be first served'.[55] As a result, the general public was forbidden to buy coal (called sea coal because it was usually transported by sea) until noon.

There was traffic congestion even then. A complaint to Master Mayor and the council from their co-citizens declared, 'High Causey about the Market House is blocked by extra stalls and so thrusted impestered and cumbered on Market days that it is sometimes very hard to pass and re-pass. The thing is not only tedious and painful to the weak and aged but also dangerous and perilous to women that are great with child and dangerous to country folk for putting down and taking up their bags'.[56] The citizens wanted the iron and fruit stalls moved to Saint Peters Square to spread out the trade.

Horses were not to be brought to the market place but left at inns or lodgings. Wains belonging to salters and others were to be parked between the Tolsey and Bysters gate over the channel. When they were moved at the end of the market, the place where they stood was to be swept clean.[57] In 1576, Gregory Prise, the Mayor, had instructions from the queen, to warn anyone coming into the city to leave their weapons at their inns except knights, esquires and `people of worship', who could have a sword borne behind them.[58]

As well as the difficulty of getting round the market place the streets seem to have been pretty hazardous for the passer-by, thanks to the obstacles left about by their fellow citizens. In 1620 John Hill was presented, at a view of frankpledge 'for keeping an unlawful mastiffe dogge soe that the kings majesties subiects cannott passe alonge the kings highe way without great danger of hurtinge' [59] and in 1624 Thomas Quarrell of St Owen's parish was presented for 'causing annoyance at the Boothall back door by putting in standard (scaffolding) poles to the hindrance of passengers that pass that way'.[60] Thomas Williams was told to fill in a sawpit 'in the high causey apud (beside) Saint Peters Cross'[61] and in 1625 Luke Hulett, gentleman was presented for not putting 'a sufficient barre or rayle at his taverne (cellar) stayers belonging to his house according to a payne put upon him at the last tourne wherefore he hath incurred the payne of ten shillings and he is commanded sufficiently to doe the same before midsomer next upon payne of twenty shillings in default'.[62] He lived in Narrow Cabbage (Capuchin) Lane.

No shops were to open or trade during divine service. Just in case anyone thought they could relax 'no one is to remain idle, sitting, standing or vagrant in the street but repair to church.'[63] The right to trade was jealously guarded. Among other privileges which they enjoyed, freemen were the only people who could carry on a trade within the city. Only they could join the powerful guilds which controlled the different trades and crafts. The records are full of their complaints about outsiders coming into the city to practice their crafts and sell goods and about residents of the city who were neither freemen nor guild members setting up in business. In 1615 the mayor received a petition from the men in the 'trade of translating or cobbling, paying scot and lot' who wanted no one who had not served an apprenticeship with a corvisor within the city and been allowed by the mayor and wardens (of the guild) of the occupation of corvisor for the time being, to be 'allowed to use the mystery or trade of translating or cobbling' because unqualified men from outside were taking their trade. And 'allsoe divers yong men that have served within this city of late refuseth to worke newe worke but setteth up shoppe for translating onely all which is the utter undoing of your petitioners. (Translating was only repairing leatherwear, cobbling was more difficult).[64] The request was allowed. In 1618 the maltsters and brewers complained that they were wronged by 'strangers and foreigners coming daily into the city to inhabit and putting up malt making and brewing here not being freemen or licensed thereto.' Any foreigners made freemen should pay five marks to the mayor, five to the chamberlain and five to mending decayed bridges and causeways 'whereof is greatest need.'[65] The butchers asked that country butchers should not be allowed to stay all night on market days.[66] William Gill, a freeman was sent to the Boothall for selling skins contrary to statute 'but obstinately refused to stay in ward and left without licence'. He was sentenced, 'to be discharged and lose his liberties and be taken as a foreigner and no freeman or free merchant.'[67]

As well as regulating the market place, the council were ordered to control prices so that the poor could afford to feed themselves. In 1587 the

Council of the Marches ordered that as there had been `great plenty of grain and corn and as there have been such hard times past for the poor they are to make sure that the assize of bread ale and beer are proportioned so that the poor sort may be better relieved'. They were to certify that this has been done by November 8th next.[68]

The Assize of Bread and Ale was held twice-yearly.

The Assize of Bread and Ale 1576;

Every baker of the city was 'to make good and hable whyte bread well and thoroughly baked'. They were to sell a penny loaf for a penny, two halfpenny loaves for a penny. No manner of grain was to be used in such bread except good clean sweet wheat. The penny loaf varied in weight according to the middle price of wheat. Three loaves of horse bread which consisted of `beans, peason and fatches' (vetch) were to cost a penny. There was a twenty shilling fine and forfeiture of all bread for each default. Forfeited bread was often given to the poor. Each baker had to put his mark clearly on the bread.

In 1619, the Mayor sent out and bought a penny white loaf and penny wheat loaf from Owen Phillips, baker, and weighed them. They were one and a quarter ounces short, so, as this was Phillips' second offence he was fined.[69]

All sellers of beer in their houses were to charge a penny for three pints. A fine of twenty shillings and forfeiture of the beer was the penalty for all defaults. It was to be sold by sealed (i.e. stamped with a seal) measures. All retailers were to sell by pottels (two quarts), quarts and pints sealed with the queens standard and 'no other newly invented measure. No hoppes or ashes were to be put in ale' one gallon of good metheglen (a spiced mead) was to be sold for sixteen pence, fourpence a quart.

According to the Customs Book, 'if any brewers sell by any measures made to the deceiving of them abiding in the city, let those measures be taken by the buyers, and brought to the bailiff of our lord the king (the Mayor).' He was to burn such measures before their door or in the most public place in the whole city. In 1605 seven men were warned to bring in their pots and vessels to have them sealed and in 1619, three people in Wyebridge ward were presented for 'keeping of unlawful measures.'

Butchers were only to sell wholesome meat and no bulls meat that had not been slayed by hounds. (It was believed that this made the flesh tender). 'No swine were to be fed with entrails of beasts nor their blood.

Tallow chandlers were to sell one pound candlelight of tallow for 4½d, butchers' tallow 2s 6d a stone, molt (clarified) tallow three shillings.

No victualler was to charge more than fourpence for two dishes of boiled meat and one roasted, a halfpenny for a footman's bed, fourpence for horse grass of the best for one day and one night, two or threepence for other grass and a penny for three pints of ale.[70]

Among the items passed from mayor to mayor were the town weights and measures. They included: A brass (mete) yard, a gallon, a quart and a pint of brass, six pieces of brassen weights, six weights of great and small troy weight with the letter 'H' engraved on them and eight pieces of leaden weights. There was also a key to the Tolsey door, one to the common coffer and one to another smaller coffer within the said common coffer.[71]

In the year of the Armada the Queen commanded that someone should be sent to London to fetch a new set of standard weights which had been provided 'as good cheap as could be had' for £9 8s 11d - in fact a considerable sum.[72]

When very few people had clocks, bells were very important, There was a complaint that the day bell had not been rung for two years making it very hard for poor people to get to work on time. It was agreed that the bells of All Saints should be rung for a half-hour at four in the morning between November 1st and February 2nd.

The Common bell was rung by the Clerk of Saint Peters at eight or nine o'clock each evening between November 1st and March 25th for which he was paid 11s 8d per annum (two shillings from the mayor 4s 8d from the chamberlains and five shillings from Widemarsh money). Anyone caught wandering about after then could be imprisoned. Only respectable citizens carrying a light should be out after dark.

In 1600, Walter Bodenham, clerk of Saint Peters, petitioned for more money, for when his 11s 8d was granted `everything was more plenty and better cheap than it is now' and he had to pay 1½d for the ringing and to repair the baldric (the leather strap which hung the clapper). The first and second inquests agreed to allow an extra five shillings the third refused.[73]

Government of the City

Despite efforts to stop people going about after dark there were still problems. In 1625 William Carwardine, Sergeant at Mace, asked for the lease of 'A voide place under the West end of the Market house stairs which nightly is defiled by disorderly people to the great annoyance of the dayly walks of orderly people there.' He promised to build a shop and pay twenty shillings rent. It was agreed that 'Viewers' should go and look at the site.[74]

On another occasion, Jenkin Phillips chief constable of Wyebridge ward 'about eleven at night produced the bodies of Richard Lloyd and William Powell for breach of the peace, fighting in an alehouse, being playing at cards. Confessed the said Powell did break the said Lloyds nose to the effusion of his blood and upon examination of them they swore many oaths'. They were committed to ward till they could find sureties to appear at the next sessions and 'until they pay three shillings each for their rash oaths'.[75]

A complaint in 1627 said that John Adams, apprenticed to John Finch, joiner, contrary to his indentures was found 'most vile drunk, lying in the street insomuch that he at the same time lost his hatt.' He attacked his master in the shop nearly blinding him. He was only saved by Mrs Finch fetching neighbours. John Adams was 'a common night walker' when he was supposed to be in bed, he broke windows to get in, so that several times a felon got in and was found lying in the hay.[76]

In what sounds like a case of teenage hooligans making someone's life a misery, John Nicholas, beer brewer, was presented before the Mayor for pulling a boy's ear and drawing blood. In reply he complained that Sybyll Webb servant to Richard Ravenhill and Mary Parker, daughter of John, disturbed him at night with others. He said the boy had beaten his son.[77]

In 1605 Richard Tornan was presented 'for kepping dysorder in his howse out of due tyme to the disturbans of his neybowers and allsoe unlawfull games.'[72]

There was no street lighting but `All inn holders, vintners, tallow chandlers and candle sellers, tippling houses and alehouses, councillors and all manner of persons that hath byn mayors, shall, from All Saints to the

Feast of the Purification of the Virgin Mary put a lantern and a candle at their doors from six till eight unless the moon is shining.' [78]

We may think the streets of Hereford are dirty now but things were infinitely worse in the sixteenth century despite the council's bye -laws, repeated at regular intervals, such as 'No citizen is to throw or emptie any chamberpot or any other unwholesome things either out of their windows or their doors into the streets at night. Whereby to make any noyesome smells to annoy the neighbours.' [79]

In 1549 Master Canon Leuson was presented for 'mantenyng hys servants to cast doges overe in to the kynges wey to nowans of the kiynges sobietes.'[80] Keen, a butcher was presented in 1596, 'for opening and dressing of fleshe in the fore street also for scalding and drawing of his pork to the annoyaunce of his neighbours'[81], despite this regulation forbidding the practice; 'butchers are not to slay any beast in the Fore street nor shed the blud of the beast in the highway ne lay any heads of beasts in the streets or highway but make it carried away forthwith upon slaughter. They must keep no entrails of beasts in their houses or shops any one night but must be taken away by night not day to Wyebridge and there to cast it in Wye at the place accustomed while they be new to avoid infection.' The fine for not doing so was 6s 8d.[82]

Everyone with timber wood or block lying in the street was to remove them before Saint Andrews Day and 'No person shall allow a dunghill muck or cley in any street over against their doors or walls but take it to the common myskyns (dung and rubbish heaps). All citizens shall keep the streets clean and channels clear before their houses. They shall not allow any swine or ducks to go at large within the gates of the city.'[83] There were legal rubbish or dung heaps but there were illegal ones as well. There was one up against the wall of All Saints church and one in Packers Lane (East-West Street). Goodknaves miskin in the area now covered by Maylords Orchard and the Portfields miskin outside Eigne Gate were two of the legal ones.

All Saints seems to have been a target for rubbish. In 1617 it was ordered that, 'the inhabitants of All Saints and all others that none of them throwe any mucke dung duste rubble or any other filth at the end of the church of All Saints nor against the walls.'[84] Two years later the church wardens had to pay 8d to have rubble removed from the church walls. This was not their only problem; in 1619 John Lane appealed for the equivalent of planning permission saying there was a piece of void ground at the end of All Saints church adjoining his house. ' There is a pump on the said piece of ground under which there is a well, as the land is so near the street many passengers goeing that way and many of the inhabitants thereabouts in making water against the said church wall doe defile the said well in making it unholesome for the kings majesties subjects to the great annoyance of the inhabitants there.'[85] He wanted to move the wall of his yard which adjoined the void ground nearer the pump to stop people making water there.

Broad Street,towards All Saints James Wathen 1799

Most people had to rely on the common pumps for their water but these were often out of order. A complaint of 1624 said `the pump next unto the Kings Ditch is out of repair, and hath been dry this half year so that from Saint Nicholas church unto the north yard almost there is no water to be had upon any necessity'.86[86] There were pumps or wells in Bridge street, Broad Cabbage Lane, Guilford street, Milk Street, where the Dean and Chapter had their dairy (now St John's St), the Market House, two in Widemarsh Street, one by Saint Peters church, one by All Saint's church and one by the Tolsey. If there were any cesspits, they would have been in the cellars, usually with no access except through the house. They would be emptied by laystow or night soil men at night. The majority of people had to dispose of their waste as best they could, often into the street like Richard Pryce and Robart Hogton, who were presented for 'anoanse of their neyborse with pys pottes'. and fined twopence.[87] Numerous people were fined fourpence for keeping illegal miskins; John Boyle for one in the king's highway,[88] Master Havard for making one behind the Boothall,[89] William Halwort for annoyance of a miskin defiling the water course[90] and Jonas Meredith for making a miskin in the back lane at his garden door in St. Owen's ward.[91] Walter Not, Richard Marcraft, John Partridge and Mawd James, were accused of 'charge of gabels to Wye fore nine of the clock.[92]

Even those who had their own privies were not always too fussy about them; Robert Jones, glover, was fined a penny for `the annoyance of a jakes (privy) kept over the water'[93] and Richard Russell 'we do leve for a jakes whyche dothe saver. We do peyne him to mend hyt by Crystmas next upon peyne of 3s 4d.'[94]

People in this period have a reputation for being dirty. The well-off could have their washing done by laundry maids like the one Thomas Hyken walked round the city wall, the less well off had to go down to the washing place at the Bargingams on the river. This was at the castle barbican east of the Vicars Choral orchard and down-stream from the bridge where the butchers were instructed to throw their waste! On the opposite bank was the watering place where farm stock would go to drink. When linen was the only lightweight material washing was a hard job particularly on cold days. For washing at home every drop of water had to be fetched, so there was some excuse for not washing too often. Clothes were hung on hedges to dry and sometimes stolen. Alice Prees was accused of stealing a sheet off Thomas Duppa's hedge in Pipe Lane (Gwynn St).[95] The accounts of St Nicholas and All Saints show that the church cloths and the surplices were washed about once a year.

Cabbage Lane, from a water colour by David Cox

Plague

The one time when strenuous efforts were made to clear up and burn the dung heaps and other rubbish was when plague was in the area. Plague seems to have occurred in a cycle of about five years. The cause was not understood and there was no cure. Very few people survived so everyone was terrified. The only way to escape was to go away from the infected place if you could, or keep anyone from infected areas out of your town. 1565and 1566 were bad years; in 1565 a letter came from the mayor and sheriffs of Gloucester assuring Hereford's mayor and citizens that rumours of plague in Gloucester were exaggerated, 'We assure you that the High Street of this whole citie have (except in one or two howses) remayned this whole yere free and though Gods blessed hand in dyvers places of the suburbs and backlands hath been felt' since Easter 'there have not dycessed above 110 persons, none in the areas of greatest traffic'.[96] So they thought Hereford should not refuse to receive their citizens.

1566 an order came from the Council of the Marches at Ludlow 'as God has visited Hereford with plague the Mayor is to proclaim that none of its citizens is to visit Ludlow or its fair'. The Mayor replied that he had made proclamation and fixed a copy of the letters on a post in the market place but after conferring with his brethren 'finds that few persons have lately died of all manner of diseases so that whosoever dyd gyve unto you any other knowledge is not a just man.'[97]

An entry in the Dean and Chapter's act book for September 11th 1563 shows that rather than worrying about their flock, they were only concerned for their own safety, ' A plague now endangering Hereford and its people now grows more and more by day. To allow a little time for it to reduce, John Ellis, Dean, Roger Stroty, Edward Cooper, Nicholas Smyth in residence greet all those considering their health and grant leave of absence from duties in the cathedral until the next Feast of Jerome' without any loss of stipend commons etc. through their absence.[98] This was continued in March 1564, 'since the plague is now in the city the Dean and Chapter announce a confirmation and continuation of the act of 11th September without penalty to all.' Later in the same year, the original act was repealed.

In 1566 Mr. Grene, a burgess, was rebuked by the Privy Council for going up to Parliament despite plague in London and being commanded not to. He received 'sharp words' from Mr. W Smyth (the writer), but he was to receive his due allowance as he had conducted himself well and 'lyke a good burgesse behavid himselfe'.[99]

One of the few means of stopping the spread of infection was to establish 'pest houses' and isolate sufferers there. In 1619, William Gwillim complained that he had been possessed of tenements in Grope Lane (Gaol Street) which had been taken and made pest houses for the sick in the last visitation. He had had nothing for them since although he had previously had £4 per annum income.[100]

The 'last visitation' he refers to may have been the one in 1610 when the parish register for St Peters for April 2nd records the burial of Hugh Daniell glover and adds ' the same day the plague began'. Between then and the end of December when there is a note. 'now the sickness ceased' there were 112 deaths nine of which are marked `not of the sickness'. In 1608 there were thirty deaths and in 1607 twenty–four. St John's[101] shows thirty-eight deaths, twice as many as any other year between 1604 and 1625 and All Saints fifty-four when there were usually less than a dozen deaths.

The church wardens accounts for Saint Nicholas show that in 1605 they received five shillings 'for the keeping of them that weare infected with the plake at St Gillis'

In 1625, the church wardens of All Saints were paid five shillings by 'Master Mayors appointment for sending back to London the woman that had the plague.' Philip Milward, a baker, was fined 13s 4d for sending a man to London when plague was there as he might have brought it back to Hereford.[102] That year must have been one when there was particular fear of plague coming to Hereford. There is the following rather odd series of entries in St Nicholas accounts;

> `Paid for a boocke for fasting and praying in the time of the plague 15d
> Paid for not having a boocke for fasting and praying in the time of the plague 2s 2d

Paid for not having a boocke for fasting in the time of the plague 7d
Paid for 2 boocks for thanksgiving after the time of the plague 2s 1d'

The likely explanation is that at that year's visitation from the Dean, he, conscious of the likely need for them, had fined the wardens for not having the service books for the time of plague and they had duly bought them.

Fire

The 1610 map probably doesn't show the houses accurately but it does demonstrate how closely packed they were along the streets. As they were mostly timber-framed, some with thatches, it is easy to imagine how quickly fire could sweep through a whole area. With no fire-fighting equipment belonging to the city, the council had to do the best it could. This is an Elizabethan bylaw:

'The mayor and every one of the aldermen his brethren, should have in his house three buckets of leather; every one of the council two such buckets; and every inhabitant, widows as well as others, being assessed in £3 or above, one like bucket at the least,. Every freeman should provide himself with a like bucket within a year after he was sworn and practised his craft. Every ward within the city should provide a ladder of thirty or twenty-four rounds at the least. To be in readiness in time of adventure of terrible fires that happen at any time within the city, to be occupied for the pacifying of all fires, Fine for all persons defective forty shillings'.[103]

The accounts of All Saints show that in 1622 they paid the considerable sum of thirty-six shillings for 'twelve buckets of leather and the caryage them to Hereford.' A wise precaution as the church stood with shops right up against its walls. By 1625 only one bucket remained.

The Custom Book says that the common bell was to be rung by the Mayor 'as well by day as by night, to give warning to all men living within the city and suburbs. We do not say it ought to be rung unless for some terrible fire burning any row of houses within the city ...... or any other calamity such as civil disturbance or a siege.'[104] Every one living in the city had to come to the Mayor to be told what to do.

After an appeal from Nantwich in Cheshire, which had been nearly destroyed by fire, the citizens of Hereford raised 58s 4d to help them, acknowledging that they had, 'cause to praise the Almighty for his long and gracious preservation of the said city and people'.[105] It is surprising that the city did escape fire when some of the citizens were so careless.

In 1625 a complaint was made about John Williams, butcher, and his wife Joan, living in the shop or house of Robert Reeves and his wife Maude from week to week at the will of the said Maude. They continually made a fire in the shop 'being a room very low neere to the solar overhead' without a chimney and mostly under a low pair of stairs from the shop to the solar, or loft, overhead so that everyone was terrified. Edward Rawlins J.P. and the Mayor had commanded them to stop, but they had carried on and, 'the said Joan, in contempt of the said mayor gave out and said she cared not a pudding for him and she would make a fire there whatever any one said'. When reproved by a neighbour she said `if she could not make a fire here she would leave her child upon the cawsy (street) to be kept by the city.' On one windy night Maude came with water to put it out and John Williams came at her with his cleaver and swore he would kill her if she meddled with the fire. Then she was scared for her house and her life. Apart from this, the William's slaughtered all their beasts in the shop next to the street within the city. They were also unruly and noisy, fighting and quarrelling in general. Although they had been given notice they said they intended to stay until '(which God forbid)' the end of their lives.[106]

William Plott, who lived in Wyebridge street, must have been alarmed by the conduct of his neighbour Walter Merricke, a baker, who was charged;

'He hath obstinately erected and made a great pile of fagots in his backside adjoining to his house within the walls of the said city to the great enormity of the neighbourhood if it be not removed.

Item, the said Merricke hath erected an oven in such a little roome of his house that when he stirreth his fyer in his oven he is constrained to carry his pole into his backside to be quenched, the same backside being adjoining unto a woodpile of William Plott gent and by that means hath byn like to endanger the said Master Plotts house of fyer. It may burn the said Master Plott in his bead, being a lame man and not able to avoid it and the said Merricke being wished to reforme the same hath denied to doe.

Item, the said Merricke pileth certaeine fagots in a lodging next the street in such a manner that he breaks down the walles of a chamber of the said Master Plotts to the great annoyance of the said Master Plot.'[107] Merricke was fined.

About 1618 Thomas Towsie and Roger Goulding complained that Richard Eysham, tanner had 'built a new house or kelling to dry his bark' near Thomas 's barn and Roger's house. 'As it is only thatched with straw it is therefore very unfit and dangerous for such a purpose because of the danger of fire'. They asked the three inquests to reform it. Eysham was told to tile his kiln on pain of a ten shilling fine.[108]

The Defence of the Realm

In times of danger to the nation from rebels within or enemies without, the sovereign had to rely on the support of the nobility with their retainers and the trained bands as there was no standing army. In theory the trained bands consisted of all able–bodied men between the ages of sixteen and sixty. They had to turn out with their weapons and what armour they had when called upon but those who could afford to often paid to avoid duty. Although the bow and arrow was being superseded by firearms, archery practice was still compulsory and each of the city wards was supposed to have a pair of butts. One of the duties of the constables was to check that they existed in good condition. In 1625 Eigne ward was presented for `wanting a pair of butts' as well as a set of stocks.[109]

The trained bands had to have training camps every year. Among the city records was a scrap of paper with a calculation of the cost, 'expenses of ten days training for the trained bands and for powder and shot: twenty bullets for the callyver of the tower is just one pound weight and one pound of powder will make twenty-five shot allowing of quarter weight of powder. To every bullet and the over-plus after that rate is five shot more, which is for touch powder and thirty shot to the pound of powder whereof five allowed for touch powder. For sixteen persons after 8d the day for ten days - £5 6 8. For ten days for powder after 16d per pound of sixteen persons £3 6 8. For bullets 29s 8½d. Towards the training about twenty shillings'[110]

In 1554 When Mary came to the throne and planned to marry Phillip II of Spain there was danger from a rebellion led by Sir Thomas Wyatt. An order was sent to the Mayor and his brethren straitly charging them and commanding them `for special reasons to have such care and regard to the keeping of the watch nightly within the city that every night there may be substantial watch kept and the same to be of the most honest sort of men and in a good substantial number, as they will answer at their extreme perils' [111]

In March 1559 a letter was received from Elizabeth, the new queen, saying that as the war begun in Mary's reign against France and Scotland was still going on the mayor was to take a general muster of the city and liberties and check weapons and armour and certify the same to the Privy Council.[112]

Later, as part of the precautions against the danger of rebellion by Catholic peers, aided by the French, in support of the claim of Mary Queen of Scots to the throne, parcels of arms and armour were sent round the country. Hereford received theirs rather informally, as the following letter from George Lodge, sergeant to the Right Honourable Sir Henry Sidney Lord President of the Council of the Marches, to one of the leading citizens shows;

'My friend Thomas Maylard,- when God shall send you to Hereford, it may please you to deliver, according to my Lord President's commission, to the mayor and his brethren these parcels following, which you have received of me as by your aquittance doth appear. First twelve corselets, six white and six black, with their furniture, such as they have, without flasks, white morions fifiteen, pike arms thirteen. This is the whole that I have delivered to you at this present, which I pray you see delivered in good order, and God be your good speede. In London, 16th April, anno 1561- George Lodge[113]

A motley collection of arms was kept at Eigne Gate. In 1578 Brian Newton armourer, was to be paid ten shillings annually for work upon them, they were ' to be scowred repared and salfelie and cleanlie keapte' They are recorded in 'a bill indented of all the harnes and armour in igne gate taken the third daie of Februarie 1579 and delivered to the charge and custodie of Brian Newton armourer as followethe:

Imprimis 7 blacke corslettes
Item 6 whitt corslettes lacking the umbraces of one of them
One blacke almaine rivett
11 morrianes
12 armed pickes
7 calivers wth 6 morrens unto them
7 flaskes & 7 touche boxes
7 arga boshes wth 5 flaskes & 5 towche boxes
3 swordes 3 doodging hafte daggers with sword girdles
8 jackes

2 halberdes 3 glives
I bowes and 20 Sheves of arrowes
5 paire splintes 3 skooles 3 sallettes
One broken paier brigandynes
2 chambers for the gret gonnes in the
Gonne-howses by the yate'.[114]

When the Armada threatened, on the ancient principle of knight service, the bishop was called on to provide one demi – lance (heavy dragoon) and one light horseman armed with a corselet and other horseman's 'stuff' and to carry a pistol.[115] In fact it seems he was armed already as in 1585 William Davies sued John Catchemaie for eight shillings for a callyver (pistol) supplied to the bishop. Catchemaie was to pay for it out of money he owed the bishop.[116]

In order to pay to fortify the coast during the long war with Spain the first state lottery was started in 1567. The prizes were articles of value, the draw taking place between January and May 1569 at the west door of Saint Paul's. 40,000 lots at ten shillings each were sold. Thomas Church and a group of councillors decided to venture £15, Thomas Church took four shares and collected the money. He covenanted with the others to divide any prizes between them according to their stakes. John Maylord, the mayor, bought one share. Whether they won is unknown.[117]

Women

At this time women had very few rights; once they were married what property they had became their husband's and he was very much the senior partner in the marriage, legally allowed to beat her. The wife was expected to be submissive towards her husband and obey him in all things. In return, he was supposed to support her and tolerate her foolish ways. Sir Thomas Smith, a sixteenth century statesman, describing the various ranks of Tudor society came down to the very lowest level before he dealt with women; 'Lastly, bonds men, be taken but as instruments and the goods and possessions of others. In which consideration also do we reject women as those of whom nature hath made to keepe home and to nourish their families and children, and not to meddle with matters abroade, nor to beare office in a citie or commonwealth no more than children and infants.' [118]

Very few of the records deal with personal relationships in marriage but here are two examples, in the first, Margaret Church, a dutiful wife, wrote to her husband to warn him of trouble;

' Swet-hart - I commend me unto the, praying god for thy healthe and prosperitie, Soule and bodie. I thank the for my moony, good swet-harte. I entret the for god's sake to rid Arkinstall out of your company as thou loves thy credit. He stolle a mare of three pounds prise coming from Westchester. I was before the mayre on sunday morning, and the man that owneth the mare was in towne and proof with him, and hath laid sirth all about the towne and countre to take him, and will hang him except he forsake England; there fore for the love of god rid him as soon as you can. Master Gillim and Master Church was the furst that told me, and would wish the to rid him, and master maire himself would wish the to have honest in thy companie and would request the to come and speke with him when thou come home. A saturday the house was seeersth for him, that we were all at our wits end. No more at this time. I shall think long tel I here from the where you hear anie thing of him; this I end

Thy loven wife, Margaret Church, tell deth.

Church was examined by the Mayor but he said Arkinsall had bought the mare so the case was dismissed.[119]

A marriage between a pair of undesirables was that of James Franken and his wife. He was, 'a very lewd dissolute and disorderly fellow a drunkard and blasphemer', who, among other things, called his neighbour Margaret Floid whore, witch and 'gowthie' whore and threatened to set her house on fire. He called the wife of another neighbour whore and his two daughters bastards and attacked his own mother. On another occasion, 'He came home drunk and found his wife drunk so struck her a grievous blow, she fell down speechless, he them took a firebrand and burnt her back. Her neighbour had to fetch claie to cool out the heat ' His wife abused one of his neighbours 'verie much in callyng her whore, mounmeth whore and not content with that but cast a chamber pot of erren in her face whereby she was likelye to be blynded'.[120]

In practice it seems that most marriages worked as a partnership and, when widowed, wives were often made executors of their husbands wills and carried on running their businesses. The only women who could own property were widows or single heiresses. For instance, in Hereford in 1624 William Baker was landlord of the Starre[121], in the next year Widow Baker of the Starre was assessed at 8d church rate, she was the poorest of ten widows assessed, the wealthiest paying 16 shillings.[122] The subsidy assessment for 1624 shows that out of 214 people assessed, 38 were women, 7 of whom were definitely given as widows and 4 as two pairs of sisters, presumably single, two, not shown as widows, had sons, probably minors.[123]

There is plenty of evidence that some women asserted themselves to the disadvantage of their fellow citizens. The Custom Book had this to say about them;

'Concerning scolding women; by them many evils do arise in the city. By wrangling fighting and defaming they trouble by night those that are at rest and oftentimes move schisms between their neighbours; contradicting the bailiff, ministers and others in their prison speaking ill or cursing them and oftentimes by their cries and clamours breaking the peace of our lord the king and troubling the tranquillity of his city. Whereupon, at all times when they shall be taken they shall have their judgement without redemption. There they shall stand with their bare feet and their hair hanging about their ears for so much time as they may be seen of all those which pass by that place, according to the will of the bailiff of our lord the king or of the bailiffs of other fees. After the judgement be finished, let her be brought to the gaol of our lord the king and there stay until she hath made redemption at the will of the bailiff whose tenant she was. If she will not be amended by such punishment let her be cast out of the city; and this by our chief bailiff with the power of the city, if needful. For divers evils and dangers may arise oftentimes by such persons and their maintainers; and if there be any such perturbers of the peace and tranquillity of the city, let it be done with them as with perjured men'.[124]

These draconian punishments had obviously not worked as there are a number of presentations of scolds in the records. Mary, wife of John Jones butcher, was presented as a 'common scold, drunkard and disturber of her neighbours and one that is a common curser swearer and blasphemer of god's name'. The great inquest found this to be true.[125] This John Jones is the likely first owner of the Old House which can still be seen in High Town when it was built in 1621, Mary, by then a widow, was still there in 1664 when she was assessed for hearth tax.[126]

'Articles exhibited against Margaret Gyles wife of John Gyles: she is a common scold & daily doth disturb her neighbours with most vile and sclanderous speeches and railings against them soe as they cannot be in quiett in their house. About a month ago she met Sibill Huntt, widow, an aged gentle woman of about 70 years, near Saint Owens Gate having a pretended malice against the said Sibill and Dorothy Giles her daughter, rushed the said Sibill from the wall into the channel and there strake the said Sibill with an eareinge blade upon her head. By reason of the said blow she fell into the gutter, and the said Dorothy coming to rescue and help her mother being down in the gutter she the said Margaret ran unto the said Dorothy forciblie and took her by the throat where upon she was in great peril of her life.

Item, the said Margaret did then and there in most scandalous and uproarious manner and with most uncivill termes call the said Dorothy arrant whore, burned whore, common whore and bastard whore and sayed that she would make her look up and set forth her bastardy. And not so contented she then and there most wilfully smacked up the mire and durte forth of the channell and did cast it in the face of the said Sibill and

Dorothy and pooled (pulled) of the band from the said Dorothy's neck and tore it all to pieces and soe continueth in her wild words not respecting any person at all in consideration of the premisses. The said Sibill and Dorothy humblie prayeth the good behavior to be granted against the said Margaret whereby they may goe about their business in Gods peace and the kings'.[127]

Anne Powell, wife of Stephen was another undesirable neighbour. She was presented 'for her lewd life, bad conversation,' and vile behaviour towards her neighbours. 'Imprimis she is a common scold and doth disturb her neighbours which for as they cannot leave (live) any day in quiet for her being so notorious vile and scandalous with her tongue. On May 2nd upon mere malice against William Yayden and his wife Margaret, her neighbours, brought forth a certain pot of stinch and threw it before the door of said Yayden to their great annoyance and the neighbours. The said Margaret Yayden reprehending her for it the said Anne Powell called her great arst, gade, get thee home and be hanged with thy neighbours and also called her thief and said her servants and maids were whoores.

On Dec 8th she threw open the pigges cot door of William Kinnersley to the intent to have the pigges of said Yayden to go into the gardens to have them killed and would have persuaded Margaret Parsons to have helped her to hunt the pigs into her own garden so the said Yayden would be sued by her husband.

On May 12th she assaulted Yayden and gave him a box on the ear using these words calling him villain thou art whoresonne villain and hanged on his leg so as he could not get from her in a great space.

On Dec 14th Anne Powell met Margaret Yayden in the street and did spit in her face and called her thiffe. [The petitioners] Humbly prayeth (in respect of these abuses and many more, tedious to repeat) she may be bound to her good behaviour so as the kings liege people may live in peace'[128].

The punishments given to these women are not in the records. One of the traditional treatments was the ducking stool but there is no evidence that Hereford had one. As well as being scolds, women were accused of other minor misdemeanours, like Elienor Gamond, widow, presented as 'a common regrater (buying up goods to sell them at a profit later, illegal at this time) and ingroser of the market in buying and selling of fish apples, pears and all suchlike commodities within the said market'[129] and Elysbethe Vycres, presented for putting hops in ale, a miskin, and swine (wandering in the street)[130]

More seriously, there appears to have been a gang of women, possibly related, engaged in stealing things which today would hardly be regarded as worth taking, but when clothes were passed down in wills and to steal anything worth more than a shilling was a hanging offence they formed quite a criminal network.

Beatrice Gough was one of a family which seemed to be at the centre of this criminal sisterhood; she, 'being examined whether she was yesterday in the garden of Gregory Ashbrooke without Bysters gate, sayeth that shee was. Being examined what goods she tooke therehence, sayeth shee tooke away one welsh yarne sheete and a smock petticoate of flanings as it was drying uppon the hedge. Being examined what she did with the said goods sayeth that the sheete she pawnd at one Thomas Price his house in the Castle Street for tenne pence and the smocke petticoate shee left with one Ales Arbeto which goods shee did cause to be delivered againe unto the said Mr Ashbrooke's mayde and further is not examined but sayeth the sheete was not pawned by herself but by one Margaret Pember alias Lewis whoe this exiat requested to pawne for her and being examined where shee had the ruff band which shee pawned to one Margaret Gyles,, sayeth that shee had it at the doore of one William ap Thomas for sixpence and is further not examined.'[131]

In 1625 Margaret Balle was accused of stealing Thomas Adam's pig. She said that Beatrice Gough brought a pig to the Balle's house to sell but they did not buy it. Gough then asked to stay there till day but Balle's husband put her out of doors and she went away with the pig but about four in the morning they heard it crying and running about the streets so she took it in.[132]

In 1616 Richard Aston, a tailor, was examined about a stolen cloak and gown he alleged was taken from his shop by Anne Gough, spinster. She confessed to stealing from his shop, seeing the door open (he said he left it closed while he went to eat): a black buffon gown wanting one sleeve, a blue cloak with a white cape, two remnants of friese and a little piece of fustian. She took it to the house of one Rulins who cut the gown to make a safeguard to sell. He offered her 16d for the cloak but never paid. When the constable came to search, Rulin's wife Katherine made Anne Gough hide the stolen goods on a stone wall behind Ellands. She wanted the accused to bring her stuff to make into clothes for her husband.[133] This Rulins seems to have been a thoroughly bad lot. In 1591 he was presented in the Dean's court for 'adultery with a certain Catherine whom he keeps as his wife while his own wife is alive'. He was summoned on the 17th September and did not appear. He later appeared and admitted that he had married Jean, daughter of Thomas Hyde and had also married Catherine. He was told to appear at the next court when he was ordered to do penance in the cathedral and in his own parish church but did not and was obviously still living with Catherine twenty-five years later.[134]

Beatrice Gough alias Waters who was accused of stealing washing hung out by Anne Barnard said she lay all night in the house of Margaret Gyles and all day until the constables apprehended her. `Asked if she was in Hungrie Street about 11 o'clock or if she stole or consented to the stealing of any lynnen out of William Thomas garden being a lynnen apron and a waistcoat denied it'.[135]

The following is only part of the very long examination of Margaret Gough, wife of Roger, for what seems a very slight offence; perhaps it was because of the family name or maybe because it was the Mayor's barn. It is particularly interesting as it shows how close the life of the country was to the city at this time. The examination was conducted by Phillip Trehearne Esq. Mayor and James Lane J.P. She was asked about where she had the barley in the muck found in a canvas bag in her house adjoining the Mayor's barn within the city. She confessed that 'about seven in the morning she put by some of the laths of the barn which is next to an outhouse of her husbands and took about half a bushell which she meant to give to her horse, she was alone except for a little girl who lived with her who stood in the out house. Examined where she had the barley in the straw, poulse and peace in the hawme which she had in her house in Castle Street she said her husband when he gathered corn in the country was wont to bring home what corn he had gathered in the day on the cart. She denyed that they came from the Mayor's barn or from his servants when they were thrashing. When she was examined what she was doing with the mayor's servants in the barn last Wednesday she said she was there entreating them to give her a little muck for her horse. They gave her some which she carried out in her apron and put in a bag where she had some other muck.'[136] The same Margaret Gough was presented at a view of frankpledge in 1619 as 'a common drunk and scould and disturbing her neighbours'[137]

Because most of these records deal with people who had fallen foul of the law, women who led quiet law-abiding lives are only mentioned in passing, like Alice Davies, who had a cow on Widemarsh and Widow Symonds who had a bay gelding. She may be the same widow Symonds who gave St Nicholas church 'one towel fringed with blue'. The St Nicholas's church wardens accounts show that two poor women were paid 6d to make clean the church and James Baker's wife was paid 16d for washing the surplice and the table cloth. These are the only records they left.

The parish registers bear witness to the tragedy of many women who bore children year after year and buried them within days or weeks, equally they record the women who had many children who lived. The birth room was the one place where women, particularly the midwife, were in charge. A successful delivery and a healthy mother and child were cause for celebration so during her lying-in the woman was visited by her 'gossips,' - friends and neighbours who brought and consumed large amount of food and drink. Phillip Trehearne 's servant questioned whether her master served meat during Lent, said, 'that there was none to her knowledge unless some was eaten by her mistress who then lay in childbed or by some company that came to see her'.[138] The parish registers for St Peters show that Phillip Trehearne married Mary Vincent in 1612. That is all we know about her, but he features frequently in the city records.

Men

Like the ordinary law-abiding women of Hereford there were many men whose only record, where it still exists, is in the parish register, but because they served in the many city offices - council servants, churchwardens, constables, officials of trade guilds etc.- as well as being tradesmen, there is far more information about the respectable male citizens. Thomas Church, the dyer and Brian Newton who worked with metals, particularly pewter, who both served as mayor have already been mentioned. There was Morgan Taylor the plumber, Thomas Caldicott, one of the bakers and a warden of the bakers company, Roger Squire, a musician and a city wait, Francis Lyde, a goldsmith, Rowland Burghfield, cook to the Vicar's choral and John Hill and John Prees two of the many corvisors in the city, both of whom did some brewing as well, to give a few of many examples.

There is of course, more information about the men who broke the law. Women's crimes were relatively petty, as we have seen, but some men stole on a larger scale. In 1549 Owen Gryfyth was presented 'for taking Thomas Davies and William Bochard in the kings highway and took money by extortion. He 'took Thomas Tromper between Richard Vicaries house and Eigne gate and took extortion' he` extorsionusly took of Robard Glover for the said Tromper eight pence.'[139]

John Turbeville, a glazier, accused of stealing a sheep, a serious offence, said he went with Thomas Herring 'to seek a pray' Herring said he would go and fetch a sheep of his kinsman, Peers who would not hang him for it so they went to a pasture within the liberties, 'Nightingale hall'. He struck it down, Herring carried it away and gave Turberville 8d and the skin, which he hid in a hedge in Wye fields.[140]

In 1624 Richard Powell who had obviously been systematically looting the house of John Hoskins Esq. was examined by Edward Rawlings and John Warden. It is worth quoting the report in full as it gives an idea of some of the contents of a comfortable home and the splendid clothes of its owner as well as the lack of secure locks.

Powell said when he went to sell the first boule (bowl) being silver and gilt of the goods of John Hoskins esq. He found Francis Lyde, goldsmith at the house of William Whitney, corvisor. At Lyde's shop he asked him to lend ten shillings on the bowl but Lyde said he would buy it so he sold it for nine shillings 'and sayeth the same was bought and sold in his shop behind his cupboard and not upon his stall next the street neither did he weigh it.'

Lyde said if he could get any more 'such commodity he would give him somewhat for it. Since that time Hoskins was in towne (? London) twice or thrice and he broke the trunk where he had the ring and also had one dozen silk points (laces for fastening clothing). Now coming to the house of Hoskins he showed all the trunks and wooden boxes or chests which he had broken and said that out of a white box he took a pair of shoes and a French hood out of another box and out of the trunk where he had the ring, one skein of gold thread and some gold pearl and a piece of taffeta out of a white box and a piece of red cloth out of another white box. He took a gold wrought cap and a gold hatband before Master Hoskins was last in town. These trunks and boxes were in a chamber over the porch. Out of another chamber he had a pair of blue stockings and from another called the green chamber a pillow bere and a fan. From a little chamber over the entry wherinto he got out of the gallery, the two bowls lying on a shelf and a pair of new Spanish leather shoes and an old shirt. From the chamber called the new chamber he took a pillow bere. He said he had been in the house ten or more times. When he brought the other silver and gilt bowl to Francis Lyde, he said he wanted the owner to come to him, so Powell 'departed away.' On other meetings Lyde asked about the owner so Powell confessed that it was John Hoskins bowl in the presence of Walter Wale. Lyde 'willed him to bring back the nine shillings and put the bowls back and shut the matter up'. It sounds as if Francis Lyde, the Goldsmith was prepared to do some dishonest dealing but got frightened when he saw the quality of the goods he was being offered. Powell said he got in by putting back a bolt of a door through a chink or hole, sometimes with a knife, sometimes a nail. He said Margery Baldwyn who received part of the goods did go to school to one Roberts a schoolmaster. He said he told her the goods belonged to Hoskins and he lay with her one whole night at the sign of the Star.[141]

At least Powell had the sense to admit his guilt but a number of wrongdoers caught with stolen goods claimed they had no idea where they came from or someone else was responsible for them. Edward Davys was one of these; when examined about what trade and means of living he had said he was a ballad seller. Asked about the brass taken in his possession which was `the brass of certain monuments of tombs within the cathedral, sayeth thet one John Glazier brought it to him desiring him to keep it for him'. He denied that he had stolen it.[142] Ann Price, widow, said on Wednesday last she lost out oft the upper chamber of her house '4 pynners one carchath (kerchief) and 2 cappes' which were found in the possession of one Phillip Lewis, a lewd fellow. He admitted the goods were found in his possession but he 'did not know where he had them.' On view of the goods Ann Price Said they were hers, worth about 2s 6d.[143]

William Thomas, labourer, was examined concerning the theft of a felt hat and a treble cipers hat band from the house of Benjamin Trehearne. He said he 'found them' in the house and took them and going over the Wye at Sugwas met a man from Worcester and pawned them for two shillings.[144]

An interesting selection of goods was stolen from Margaret, wife of Walter Hunte, furrier, who brought Roger Watkins before the mayor accusing him of taking them. She said that on Saturday night last after market, she 'made fast the doore and windoes of her shoppe'. When she came back on Monday morning she found she had lost `two muffes for gentlewomen, certeine silver heare cony skins certeine white lambe skyns with certeine garden seeds, viz. Thyme seeds, rosemary seeds, savery seeds and margeram seeds to the value of five shillings or thereabouts.' The son of William Bowyer brought a muff to sell; asked where he got it he said he bought it of Watkins. When Watkins was found he brought another muff and said he found them in the Market House. Asked if her shop was broken Margaret Hunte said she could not tell.[145] Crimes of violence were predominantly committed by men. In 56 cases named as affray only one, which appears to be a scrap between two housewives, was committed by women, although there were cases of husbands and wives involved together, usually attacking another couple.

Officers of the law were particularly vulnerable to attack. Richard Cole, a tailor, attacked Thomas Probyn, constable when he came to arrest George Partrich, one of his workers, the same Partrich who had been accused of murdering Anne Parsons. As a result of his master's intervention he escaped.[146] Harry Flacher, sergeant, was attacked by Morgan ap Rees when he was arresting him.[147] When William Luston, a clerk, died the mayor Thomas Davies and Edward Threlkeld J.P. went to view his body but, 'they were violently thrust out' by James Parry Esq. and others armed with daggers and a hatchet.[148]

'Thomas Williams of the Citie of Hereford weaver' seemed prepared to attack anyone; he was, `a Common drunckard and Common quarreller and disturber of the Kinges Majesties peace.

Item hee made an assault and affray upon James Willcocks upon sundaie night last and did teare his hands from about his worke. Whereupon the said James Willcocks charged the Constable with him, the Constable beinge Thomas Smyth, whoe takinge hould upon him to bringe him before an officer the said Constable required the said James Wilcocks to ayde him whoe did offer to ayde the Constable and thereupon the said Williams did newly assault and stricke the said James Willcocks and the said Constable and did tourne the Constables dublet almost of his backe abusinge them both with most lewd speeches.'

`Item the said Williams upon wensdaie night last did make an assault and affray upon John Howells in Blackmarston and did beate him sore and threw him downe into a sawpit there and offered to knocke him and the sawyers there with the sawyers axe in the heades and there was soe outrageous that they were inforced to binde him hand and foote and to carrie him in a carte before Mr Mayor.

Item sithence his commitment into the gate (Bysters) hee hath given forth that when he shalbee at libertie hee will fire the howses of the said James Wilcox and John Howells or doe them some further mischief or else steale their horses.'[149]

A dangerous use of a gun was recorded when Richard Jauncy was presented `for shooting in a peece at piggons within the liberties of the said cittie'.[150]

Katheren Baughan, `Wydowe of thage of lxvje yeares or there aboutes' was one of several witnesses to a murder. She said she was sitting in her door with Joan Tyther wife of William Tyther when she saw Tyther `caminge over the streete And went into a backe lane there and as he went by this examinant shake his knife in the sheethe which he had in his hand' at her `then toke yt at his wyffe,..... and then went into the house of one Anne Hurdman wydowe and there stayed aboutes halfe a quarter of an ower and then cam agayne into the streete where this examinant was sittinge in her owne dore'. She requested Tyther to put up his knife which he had drawn in his hand but he went to the other side of the streete with his knife `to the wyndowe of one Anne Jenkins wydowe and said who is the proudeste Champion, come out of this stewes, (brothel) meaninge the said Anne Jenkins howse, to me and I will fytte him and then with his knife did cutt aboutes three twigges of the wyndowe and there uppon Edward Webbe cam furthe of the howse some what drowselie from sleepe as this examinant takethe yt with a ffaggott sticke aboutes a yard & an halfe longe to the said Tyther and said who is yt that swaggarethe here, And immediatlie strake the said Tyther uppon the showlder one blowe dangerous and there uppon the said Tyther toke houlde of the one ende of the ffaggote stick, and thruste him the said Webbe into the lefte breste with his knife with the other hand that the bludd in greet aboundance yssued out and yet not w(i)th standings the said Webbe pursued the said Tyther gevinge him other blowes as this exaiant thinkethe and shortlie the said Webbe fell downe deade.' It sounds like a tragic end to a drunken brawl. If found guilty Tyther would have been hanged.

Although it was not illegal for masters to beat their servants Thomas Church, the dyer and leading citizen, went too far. In 1619 Thomas Lucas, his apprentice, complained about his bad treatment. His master beat him, broke his arm, insulted him, broke his head in eight places, beat him with 'a great staff as much as he could grip and a bulls pizell* and his keys'. Lucas asked to be released from his bond or be apprenticed to someone else, he had already served 7 years. This was granted.[151]

The impression the last two chapters may give is that Hereford was a lawless, violent society, but, although incomplete, the records cover a period of 75 years so probably things were no worse than they are now. It has to be remembered that petty pilfering was often done to obtain necessities, not drugs, as is often the case now. Katherine Lewis who petitioned to be released from prison as she had six children must have been desperate. She was accused of stealing a piece of beef valued at three pence. (A half day's wage for a labourer).[152]

*Bull's penis, used for carrying out a flogging. O.E.D.

Schooling

Most people were illiterate; for poor people there was little chance of going to school both because education had to be paid for and working people could not afford to lose their children's labour. Many children went to school for part of the year and then went to work during harvest or other busy times so never made a lot of progress. Writing was not started until the child could read so some of them never got that far. Tradesmen and any one who wanted to rise in society needed to read and write and do simple arithmetic. In Hereford most of the officials could at least sign their names but most of the people presented for misdemeanours made their mark. The churchwardens accounts show payments made for writing up the parish registers and the accounts themselves as do the accounts for Widemarsh. These were complicated records which needed to be kept up to date so the churchwardens and the keepers of Widemarsh must have been able to do this although not all of them are signed by the churchwardens like these for All Saints.

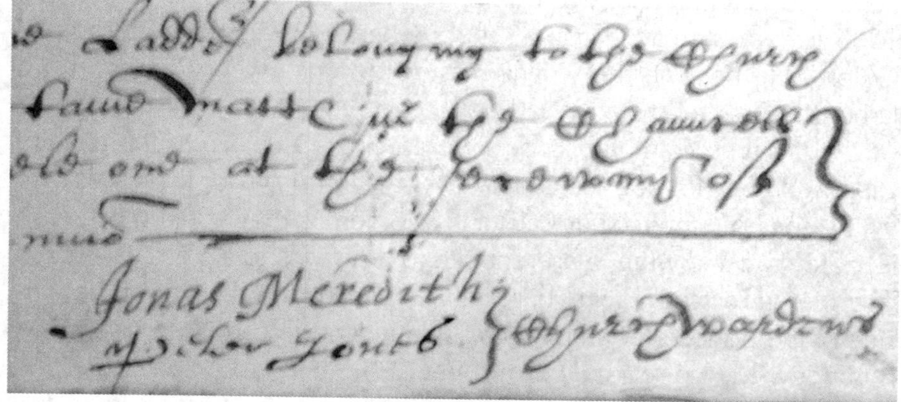

Jonas Meredith

Before the Reformation chantry priests ran small schools for boys and sometimes girls as well but most of these went when chantries were abolished. A survey of chantry land made in 1547[153] shows that the incumbent of St Owens, aged 80 was, `a right honest man indifferently (adequately) learned and taketh pains in keeping of a school and bringing up children' but there are no records of any other schools except that there must have been one in Olde Schoole Lane. There had to be some sort of schooling for young children after the reformation so the children of tradesmen etc. could learn enough to carry on their businesses. Teachers were supposed to be licensed by the church but the records of the Dean's Court show that in 1608 John Lewis in Saint Martins, William Parrott in Saint Peters and William James in Saint John's were presented for 'teaching school' without a licence so it seems unofficial `petty' schools were filling the gap left when the chantries were suppressed.[154] Surprisingly, Margery Baldwin, the 'hoore' kept at the Starre by William Baker was said by one of her customers to have gone to school with 'one Roberts a schoolmaster.'[155]

Evidence of the origin of the Cathedral School is fragmentary but in 1384 Bishop Gilbert appointed a head master to an existing school 'to govern the boys with birch and rod'.[156] Where exactly the school buildings were is uncertain. The school was to be free for boys born within the city and its liberties but the endowment was inadequate. Even so several old boys gained positions requiring a high level of education. John Davies, described as a penman, was one of the most successful; he was born in 1565 and would have left the school when he was about 15 to go to Oxford. He became the writing master to Prince Henry, eldest son of James the First, who died in 1612.[157]

At this time grammar schools were being set up across the country, supposedly free for poor boys. However the trend was for the places to go to the sons of better-off artisans and yeomen as they could more easily learn to read and write, a prerequisite for entrance to a grammar school. The Hereford school's first building was possibly on the site of the west side of the Bishop's cloister which surrounded the Lady Arbour and was burnt down in the reign of Edward VI.

In 1574 the Dean and Chapter petitioned the Queen for a free grammar school to be provided in Hereford to educate the boys of South Wales as Shrewsbury did for North Wales. Nothing was done until in 1583 when the new Cathedral statutes said;

`Concerning the school, it should be maintained as in the past within the precincts of the Cathedral church and be governed by the Dean and Chapter.' The headmaster's stipend of £13 6s 4d was increased to £20 and the usher's from £6 14s 0d to £10. 'Towards which payments the distribution (to the canons) on certain festivals, of St Milburgas loaves called simnels, with the pence anciently called mass-pence (the payment to have a mass said) shall be given, anything needed more to be paid out of the common fund of the chapter'

The Dean and Chapter were to choose the boys to have free education. The Queen's commissioners appointed Master Mey as headmaster as he was highly recommended. They asked the Dean and Chapter to 'make choice of some other godly and painful man to be usher, whom you shall think good.'[158] They reminded them to make ready the house for their lodgings but the schoolmaster and usher were lodged in the college of the vicars choral as were Thomas Cooxy schoolmaster in 1590 at a cost of ten shillings annually[159] and Mr Povey who was granted commensality, or the right to live and eat in the college, in 1595.[160] In 1587 the vicars granted William Woode, a schoolmaster from Sherborne, a lease of a property in Broad street jointly with Tho mas and Blanche Morrys . He became master of the choirboys and in his will of 1609 when he was described as master of the free school of Sherbourne he left land in Dorset valued at £10 per annum to the poor of Hereford.[161] In 1619 Thomas Smith and John Jones , both schoolmasters, were living in the city.[162]

Shortly after the appointment of Mr Mey a letter was sent to the Archbishop setting out the general discontent of the parents in the church, city and county at the incompetence of the schoolmaster and usher, 'who teach by no method set down by public authority but only by imitation, many have taken their youth away.'

There were seven choristers who were educated in the choir school but who could enter the grammar school when their voices broke. According to the act book of the Vicars Choral Mr Farant, the organist, was the master of the children and a room was set aside for them in the college.[163] At a visitation of the college in 1584 Thomas Evans and William Hosier reported that 'the choristers are not taught well' and Hosier and Bartholomew Mason said that 'they do not behave well in divine service'.[164] In 1607 Charles Langford, the Dean, willed the school his 298 acre farm at Disserth yielding an income of £30 per annum to maintain four scholars at the school. The boys were to be born within the city and be chosen by the trustees. They were to attend divine service in the choir of the cathedral wearing gowns and surplices.

The school was also left a house in Hightown- on the left-hand side of Church Street (Cabbage Lane) in 1615 by Richard Philpotts, the Mayor, to maintain two Langfordians at Brasenose College.

All grammar schoolboys learnt Latin; many of the council records, including the mayors accounts, are in Latin so some council officers were probably old boys. The Vicars Choral however seem not to have been so well educated in 1588 at a visitation by the Dean[165], Bartholemew Mason reported 'there is a library and a number of old books therein safely kept, but to little proffitt of anye, for that the mostparte do not understand the lattine tongue; but if anie of yor worship do want anie of the said bokes, we would verie gladly exchange for some newe wriiters, whereby we might be occupied in godly study, the which bokes for want of abilitie (money) they are not able to by'

There would have been about forty boys at the school who would have started at seven years of age able to read and write. The presence of a `ballet seller' in the city suggests that enough people could read to make it worth his while, but the fact that he stole from the cathedral may mean that trade was not good.[166]

A detailed study of the records would give a better idea of the level of literacy although not everyone who signed their name could read or write anything else.

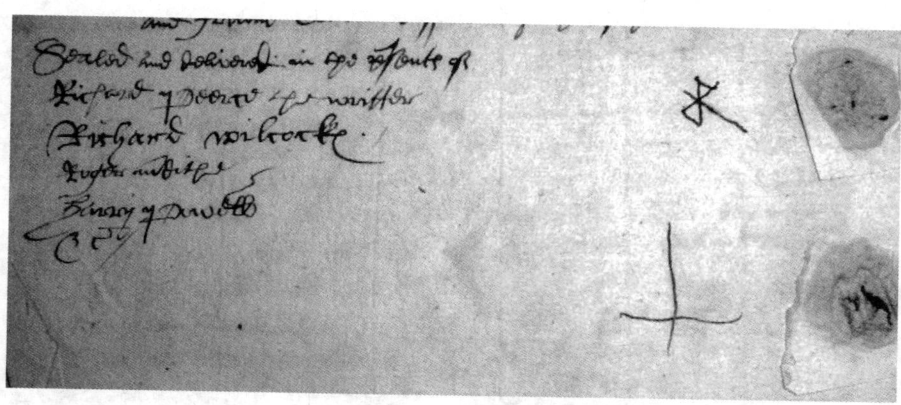

Sealed and delivered in the presence of
Richard Peerce the writer
Richard Wilcocke

The marks, with seals, of John Bramwiche butcher and John Barnes on a deed acknowledging a debt of five pounds to Thomas Wilcox. The signatures of the witnesses include that of Richard Peerce who wrote the document.[167]

The Parish Churches

St Nicholas Church, demolished 1841

There were six parishes in Hereford at this time; All Saints, Saint Peters, Saint Nicholas, Saint Martins, Saint Owens and Saint Johns which has its altar in the Cathedral. Only two sets of church wardens accounts exist for this period, those for Saint Nicholas from 1619[168] and for All Saints from 1601.[169] They each consist of an account of income and amounts spent. All Saints have long lists of parishioners who contributed to the upkeep of their church, the totals being far greater than the amounts raised in St Nicholas parish where the average years income was just over £4. In a survey of chantry land made in 1547 St Nicholas' housling (number of communicants) was given as 610 and All Saints as 600.

The expenses of both parishes show regular payments for bread, wine and candles and to the ringers for ringing the bells. The bells were in constant need of care, every year at least one of them had to have a new baldric of white leather (leather cured without changing the natural colour). The clocks, too, needed regular maintenance.

In 1621 Saint Nicholas 'paid john church for mending the wheels and the new hanging of our bells thirty-three shillings', 5s 6d for mending the clock' a clapper for the second bell, five shillings, a spring for the clock, 6d, oil for the bells and the clock, 4d and a rope for the little bell. Similar payments were made over the years by All Saints.

Roger Wolfe and John Bougham, church wardens for Saint Nicholas embarked on a programme of repairs and improvements in 1609, the payments included;

Paving stones for the church	6 shillings
Sand to pave the church	3d
Setting up a gutter	4d
Silk and thread and for the maken a cushion for the communion table	8d
Painting and making of the posts of the church green	5 shillings
Whiting the church	12d
For making new seats	22s 2d
Boards for the seats	15d
Paving the church	2s 4d
Paid to the tiler	2 shillings
Cramps and nails for the seats	12d
A seam of lime	15 shillings
(Seam – a packhorse load)	
Nails to mend an old seat	2d
Paid for a bolt and staples for the back door of the church and for four cramps	2s 2d
Lead to fasten the cramps	6 shillings

Another seam of lime to make up the walls of the church	8d
A load of clay for that work	8d
Paid to the mason for his work	8s 6d
Paid to the labourer for his work	13d
Making the church clean	3d.

In 1625, despite, or maybe because of, work done on it in 1622, the steeple of All Saints suffered a major collapse. The first indication of this is this entry in the churchwardens' accounts;

'Paid to Gullafor for crampes and great nayles for to mend one of the side walls of the church which was broken by the fall of the steeple, 2 shillings'. After this the accounts show that there was a huge amount of work to be done. Mr Lane of Ross was paid eleven shillings to 'viuwe the steeple at master mayor's appointment' so the council were concerned as well. Mr Lane was presumably a master builder or surveyor but he is not mentioned again.

From September 24th to December 10th workmen were being paid regularly, Thomas Tompson and his man were the highest earners, Tompson getting 2s 6d per day and his man 1s 6d. They were probably steeplejacks as towards the end of the work they were paid 20 shillings 'at the parishe apointement towards theire hurte when they fell from the steeple'. The other workmen were paid between 9d and 1s 2d a day. Three workman were paid 12d for 'Razinge in the stone that fell from the steeple into the bell house'.

Among the materials bought was a large quantity of rope and cord of various thicknesses and weights. As a lot of this was left among the church goods at the end of the year it was possibly used for climbing the steeple. Certainly a 'winde' costing 14s 2d and taking five days carpenter's work had been constructed from poles and standards (scaffolding) to haul stone up the steeple and this too remained among the church possessions.

Forty–six loads of stone, sand, lime, and 378 pounds of lead were among the building materials used plus hundreds of clamps (to strengthen the joints between the stones) and 195 wedges (probably shaped stones). Pins and cramps were made by John Gullofer from old iron. It must have been with some relief that the churchwardens came to the time when they paid Brian Newton £2 for making the weathercock and two shillings to have it painted red and, eventually, on December 10th, paying Hugh Trehearne 'to helpe sett up the bould spindle and weather cock'.

Apart from the responsibility for this constant round of repairs the wardens had to make a presentment to the Dean each year. None for this period now exist but they were required to answer a series of questions about the state of the church fabric, the morals of the parishioners, their behaviour during services and whether they took communion regularly. Even the suitability of the vicar could be commented on. The occasion of the presentment seemed to require some entertaining or maybe Dutch courage. In 1619 All Saints wardens paid 12d to Arthur Page for writing their presentment and 16d for a quart of burnt sack.

As burials for the whole city took place in the Cathedral cemetery the parish clergy did not collect any burial fees but the churches collected four pence for the loan of a pall or twelve pence for a black cloth. Both Saint Nicholas and All Saints owned a bier, which would have been used to either wheel or carry bodies to the cemetery. All Saints paid 16d to have theirs mended in 1619 and Saint Nicholas bought a new one for 8s 6d in 1625.

Simple funeral processions must have been a common sight in the city streets. The charges for burial at this time were 3s 4d, 6s 8d and £2 depending on how close the grave was to the altar. The Cathedral accounts show that in 1615/16, Mr Vaughan vicar of All Saints was buried for 3s 4d and in November 1618, Mr Robert Warock parson of St Nicholas was buried at a cost of 6s 8d.[170]

A terrier (survey of land and property) of 1614 for All Saints shows that it had, 'A vicaredge house conteyninge twoe bayes of buildings, a kitchen garden and backside thereunto belonging', the tithes on thirteen plots of land and those on all the gardens and orchards within the parish field and `The herbage (right of pasture) of certain pastures and meadows betweene the highway leading towards Ailston and Barrs Court in the tenure of Phillipp Trahearne gent, David Bowen, Thomas Morris ,Henry Mellin and Johan Thomas widdowe.'

Saint Owens in 1615 had a `parsonage house and a garden thereunto belonging', the tithes on five plots of land and `all oblations and offerings and the tieths of all land, home closes gardens and orchards within the said parish.' So as well as his house, the incumbent had an income from at least part of the tithes.

The Vicars Choral

The Vicars Choral were appointed to act as deputies for the Canons when they were away from the Cathedral. They were also known as `singing men' as they sang in the choir. According to their Chapter Act Book they had to demonstrate their singing ability before they were appointed. They lived a communal life and had to be ready to attend services in the Cathedral. After the reformation several of them were married so they possibly only lived in the college when they were to sing in the choir. Originally they had to attend services during the night but this was stopped by the Injunctions of Edward VI in 1547.

Unlike other cathedrals their stipends were not paid by the canons for whom they deputised but by the Dean and Chapter. Revenues from Diddlebury and Lugwardine were set aside in the thiteenth century to provide for them. In 1384 after an attempt by some of the vicars to obtain the revenues of the church at Westbury their right to hold property was disputed. This was resolved in 1395 when they were incorporated as a college, with its own seal, by Richard II. The college was able to hold property and the vicars had the right to elect one of their number as custos (warden).

From 1487 the Pope, because of their poverety, allowed the vicars to hold benefices without residing in them, so that they each had an income. In addition to this provision for individuals the college owned a considerable number of properties in the city, particularly in Castle Street. Outside the city they owned land at Bartonsham and Breinton.

In the late fifteenth century the vicars complained that in their college in Castle Street they resided 'so distant from the church that through fear of evil-doers and the inclemency of the weather, many of them cannot go to the church at midnight to celebrate divine service.' In 1472 the bishop granted them the site of two canonical houses to build a new college with twenty-seven two-roomed houses and a cloister leading into the Cathedral.[171]

Walking through this college today it is very difficult to imagine what it must once have been like. Now the vicar's chambers are offices, there are no servants bustling about, very little noise, no smells. The last of the vicars has gone but we are left with their act books, now in the Cathedral Library[172]. These are the minutes of their chapter meetings which dealt with leases, their own discipline, regulation of their servants wages and other domestic affairs but nothing of religious matters. The first is a 17th century copy beginning in 1575.

Some of the leases have extra interest; in 1578 Catherine Darnell was granted the lease of, `a house and garden in Castle Street called the Old College (no29) and two little houses on the west side, also one barn without St Andrews (St Owens) Gate adjoining to a garden appertaining to Cawkbridge vicarage. She shall sufficiently and town-like build a fore front upon the old building from the hall door or porch of the said college unto a back gate upon the east side of the said college'. Some leases were granted to individual vicars who re-let them. Others went to their clerks and their servants, in some cases when they retired.

By comparison with that of an average citizen, life in the college was very comfortable. The chimneys demonstrate that there must have been good fires. Some at least of the vicars had their own 'wood houses'. In 1583 Sir Thomas Hosier agreed to exchange his for another on condition that his original one was used as a store for the college. In a lane at the back of the college were the stables, which were for the vicars to rent. The well was in the courtyard - almost a 16th century en-suite- and some of the chambers had privies. In 1605 Dr Delabere was granted a chamber under the lecture readers chamber on condition that he replaced the old privy with a stairs. The college had its own kitchen, brewhouse and bakehouse with a water supply. In 1619 Morgan Taylor the plumber was granted a lease in Cabbage Lane 'in consideration of a leaden cistern and of other works in leaden pipes whereby water is conveyed unto the buttery and kitchen'.

Members of the college dined and supped together in their own dining hall, in addition they were entitled to an allocation of beer and ale to be collected from the buttery. The act books show an on-going effort to ration the amount and the times at which it was to be taken. The chapter proceedings show further evidence of a comfortable life in college. Tenants of the Hide Farm had to provide two bushels of charcoal daily from All Saints to Easter as well as two fat capons. A large proportion of the leases included fat hens and capons as part of the rent so the college ate well on the feast days when they were due. In 1582 George Wishart, the cook, was granted the college gardens. He was 'to provide all such herbs and potherbs belonging to the kitchen'. His yearly fee was 13s 4d; for this he was to keep their hopyard and saffron field at his own cost and charge. The vicars were to have free ingress and egress and their share of all the fruits and flowers according to custom. A very pleasant arrangement for them. `Potherbs' were vegetables, there is no refernce to the use of herbs as medicnes or to an infirmary; it would be interesting to know if there was one.. Later Wishart's fee was raised to 12s 6d quarterly to cover his wages and his servant. No doubt he would have been able to supplement this by the sale of surplus produce. In addition, in 1575, he had been granted the lease of a house in Cooken Row, occupied by his father-in-law and in 1577, a tenement and garden in Castle Street. The vicars obviously valued their cook.

Two other leases provide for payment in kind as well as money. Henry Price, a glover, had to make each vicar and the custos a pair of gloves as an entry fine. The Nyle family were granted a tenement and garden in Wyebridge St. with an entry fine of 48 ells (60 yards) of dulas (dowlas - a coarse kind of linen), the rent also included two fat hens.

On entry to the college each vicar was to provide eight bushels of good wheat and fourteen of good summer barley. It seems they had not been doing so. It would perhaps not be easy to obtain unless they happened to have it as part of their tithes. In any case, 'it had been omitted by the negligence of the custos of late days', so, in 1581 it was agreed that every vicar should bring sureties for his corn. Those who had left were to be sued by letter of attorney. This met with little success as in 1583 five vicars (out of twelve) and a clerk covenanted that by next midsummer they would enter into a bond to pay their corn within the next two years. Their chapter clerk was paid his fee in bushels of corn; perhaps he had to wait as long to get it.

The college domestic buildings must have been very attractive as a source of warmth and food to anyone in genuine need or just on the scrounge. Chapter was regularly ruling to restrict the number of servants to be in the kitchen, brewhouse and bakehouse and to exclude children, boys and dogs (and wives where possible). Restrictions were repeatedly placed on the amount of food to be taken from the table. The custos and vicars could only give to 'the allowed poor and servants of the vicars'.

The grant of commensality (living among the community) was a privilege, which had to be carefully allocated. The charge was four or five pounds yearly for the servants' table and about seven pounds at the vicars' table. Visiting 'singing men' and their servants and the vicars' tenants could be brought as guests but the steward had to be warned. Any defaults were charged at two pence for supper and three pence for dinner.

Tenancy of the comfortable chambers in the quadrangle was also much sought after. After having a number of requests for chambers backed by dignitaries they could not refuse, chapter concluded, in 1580 'that noe prebend or any other whatsoever shall have a chamber in the cloister'. In 1583 they reserved thirteen of the choicest chambers to their own election. Rents varied from 6s 8d to 13s 4d annually.

As well as not producing their entry corn many of the vicars did not pay their commons (charge for food and drink). In 1583 chapter ruled that 'if they did not bring sufficient sureties to enter into bonds for the payment thereof by this day sennight they are to pay twelve pence.' If they still did not pay for another week they were to pay another twelve pence.

In 1582 a royal commission was appointed under Whitgift, then Bishop of Worcester, to investigate the affairs of the Cathedral. They restricted the number of vicars choral to twelve and bound the officers of the college to keep the statutes without innovation (which suggests that there had previously been innovation). They found that 'for lack of good government the college is fallen into great debt especially by the excessive spending on ale and beer.' The commissioners ruled that the amount of malt used was to be limited to fifty quarters yearly; the claviger (treasurer) was to be punished if this amount was exceeded and pay for the excess. The next chapter repeated previous restrictions on the allowance of ale and beer.

According to their statutes, the vicars chosen by 'the pricker of sute of choir' and the seven boy choristers were to be present at cathedral services to sing in the choir and perform the complicated rituals. They were also to avoid 'suspect' women, swearing, blasphemy and 'sclandrous and unfryutefull talkinge' at mealtimes. From the act book it is clear that all these rules were broken continuously, despite fines and threats of deprivation.

The longest of several entries about vicars and their relations with 'suspect women' concerns the examination of Sir* James Barkstead, Sir William Hosier and Sir Thomas Ganderton about a woman found in the chamber of Richard Mason on October 29th 1581. This is the tale they told. First, Barkstead said, Mason was visited by an old man; during this time the chamber door was left open. When he came out a 'suspect woman' went in and 'he made fast his open door.' Instead of keeping quiet about it, Barkstead called Hosier who asked to go into Barkstead's bed chamber next door so he could see or hear what the couple did. They both went in and saw the couple on the bed (through a chink in the wall?) Hosier knocked on Mason's door and got no reply. Eventually, the door was opened after Barkstead banged on his chamber wall. Hosier went in, followed by Barkstead and Ganderton and asked where the woman was. Mason said there was no such woman. Barkstead then opened the stairs door and there was 'the suspect woman hid upon the stairs'. Mason was fined 3s 4d although he still denied there was any such woman.

Several of the vicars, including Hosier and Ganderton, were fined, 'sconced' for not attending chapter. If any of them missed morning prayer without giving notice to ' the pricker of sute of chore', they were fined. Sir William Hawkyns who was sworn in before his brethren in 1576 seems to have had difficulty conforming. He was soon fined four pence for not keeping silent in the dining hall and two pence for not appearing in chapel. More seriously he was charged in 1578 with revealing secrets of the college. 'He went to Mr Mydstones house at the Swan and told his wife something he had read in a letter of the Lord President and advised her to write to the said lord' (in some private matter). Despite his misdemeanours Hawkyns was, in 1579, appointed steward of the garner - storing all the corn and collecting all those chickens, presumably.*

In a community like the college there were bound to be some bad feelings, which sometimes came to the surface. In 1580 Sir Thomas Lyde

* Sir; title given to ordinary non-graduate priests

was fined five pence for saying in open hall to Sir William Vicary at the table that 'he was a seditious man, not only here but among the masters'. Later Sir Thomas Kyo was fined 2s 11d for defaming Sir William Davis' wife to his face, 'with such filthy speeches as are not to be named'. William Evans was deprived in 1601 for 'many misdemeanours in laying violent hands on Humphrey Weston in the cloisters and drawing blood.'

Despite their comfortable lives in college the vicars still reckoned that they were poor. They were not supposed to go into the town alone but to take a servant with them. At the 1595 visitation George Allen said they did not have any servants to accompany them to town as they were supposed to. Thomas Mason reported 'we have enough to do to keep ourselves wives and children. None of us are able to maintain one.' (a servant) There were complaints of a small and beggarly allowance for lights. This was made the excuse for some sort of disturbance at Christmas because of no lights when 'some half were drunk or drowsy.'

One of them gave a rather sad summary of the work of the vicars in the choir, `Our singing and songs are as they are in all other cathedral churches but what devotion or pity they stir up in the minds or the hearts I know not.'[173]

The Church

As well as being an important religious official, the bishop at this time had considerable secular powers. A large part of the city and suburbs was under the control of the bishop and the dean and chapter This was their fee which is often referred to as the Bishop's fee. Here he was entitled to have an assize of bread, wine and beer and the sealing of all weights and measures, hold his own courts and have his own prison. His tenants were to be allowed to buy and sell within the city, free from all tolls. Over the centuries this division of authority in the city had led to many disagreements with the city council and even violence. The settlements had usually favoured the bishop. Elizabeth had confirmed his privileges in 1563. However, this did not end the disputes as in 1607 Bishop Bennett wrote to the mayor and his brethren. He launched straight into his complaints; `you have lately committed many prejudices to my liberties in Hereford, and many violences to my tenants there' .... you have called for the bailiff of my fee, drawn him to your court, imprisoned him and resolved to bind him over to his good behaviour.' After listing a string of infringements of his privileges he accused them of acting contrary to their own charter and assured them that he knew their charter and would bring them `back again within the compass of their own right.' He demanded that the keys of the city should be given to his bailiff during the time of his fair. Finally he threatened to withdraw his hand from the city. The mayor and aldermen replied in very respectful tones `could your lordship vouchsafe to condescend so low as to look into the sincerity of our hearts', he would find that the accusations against them were untrue. They referred to `the time of your bountiful and gladsome residence here' but despite these and more ingratiating phrases they would not budge, saying `as for delivering up the keys of our city, or forbearing the watch of our city at any time we humbly pray at your lordship's hands a favourable construction of an absolute denial'

The exact limits of the bishop's fee are unknown and have been for a long time. After yet another attempt to settle a dispute in the eighteenth century it was suggested that enquiry should be made as to the exact extent of the fee and the result put into the court. There is no evidence that this was ever done. Part of the problem was that although in the first instance the fee was within a boundary possibly marked by two ditches running north to south (see map) over the years houses and property left to the bishop and the dean and chapter became included in the fee. This left a jigsaw of ownership which often led to conflict between the bishop and the mayor and council. In the thirteenth century it was ruled that such properties were not in future to come under the jurisdiction of the fee although the rents belonged to the bishop. The best evidence of its extent is in a survey of the Canons Fee made in 1619. Although the fee is often referred to as the Bishop's Fee it was originally the fee of the Bishop and the Canons (Dean and Chapter). In his introduction to Cantilupe's Register Canon Capes says that the part of the fee inside the city liberties became known as the Canons Fee so it seems reasonable to suggest that this survey is of the same thing. There were 198 residents living in Broad Street, Cabbage Lane, High Street, Castle Street, Bridge Street, Beyond Wye (St Martin's Street) etc., an area which would be the logical place for the Bishop's Fee to be. Even at this time Marie Price and Elenor Allen living in Broad Street weren't sure that they lived in the Canons Fee, Marie Price saying she had paid her rent to the king.

A further privilege granted by the crown to the Bishop was St Ethelbert's Fair. This had been granted to him in the twelth century, originally for three days but later extended to nine. During the time of the fair which started on May 19th and was centred on Broad Street within his fee, the Bishop had control of the city. The keys were handed to his bailiff who called all the residents to come and attend him as he rode round the fee and all the city gates with a mace carried before him and a retinue of horsemen to proclaim the fair. It was declared lawful for all persons to come to the fair after paying tolls at the gates. All weapons were to be left at inns or lodgings and booths or standings erected during the fair were to be pulled down and the spoil carried away afterwards At each gate the bailiff appointed a porter sworn to serve the Bishop for the nine days. He took over all the gate tolls and the tolls of the market, pitching pence and all standings erected on the high causeway. All trade in the city was to take place at the fair not in private houses. The bishop claimed the right to imprison miscreants taken during the fair in his own prison. As he could not impose any kind of physical punishment prisoners guilty of serious crimes had to be handed over to the mayor. A deed of 1554 witnessed that James Gill, a labourer taken into custody by the bishop's bailiff during Saint Ethelbert's fair for killing John Brown had been handed over to the Mayor Hugh Wolfe, after being in the bailiff's custody for 3 months and 3 days.[174]

As well as his power in the city, shared with the Dean and Chapter, the Bishop was one of the great landowners of the Marches having a considerable number of manors in Herefordshire and other counties as well as a London house.

Another conflict in which successive bishops were engaged was with the Dean and Chapter. Originally at the founding of the cathedral, they had been a community of priests led by the bishop but gradually, over the centuries the priests had developed into an independent body of canons led by the dean. They had become responsible for the running of the cathedral while the bishop concerned himself with the diocese. By the thirteenth century, the Dean and Chapter were denying the bishop the right to conduct visitations of the cathedral.

In 1561 Bishop Scory decided to assert his right to make a visitation. The Dean and Chapter's act book[175] has a copy of the correspondence between them, the Bishop and Matthew Parker, the Archbishop of Canterbury, in which they refused, very deferentially, to allow that either the bishop or the archbishop had any right to carry out a visitation of the cathedral. They said in effect that they had documents to prove this and were searching their archives for further proof. Matthew Parker, who had also been searching his records, rebuked them saying that he found no evidence that any of their predecessors had ever refused either his or the bishop's visitation. He said `it maketh me to suppose the worse of you as though ye would lyve without lawe, not chargeable to any reformacion in any misdemeanour ye myght be charged with'. The canons still refused and the archbishop seemed to have no power to force them to allow his visitation.

Bishop Scory demanded, a `resolute answer if you will accept me as your ordinary or no'. The answer, well wrapped up, was still no, `we be most assured by the judgement of those that be wyse and learned that we have competent matter in lawe and conscience to stand to the reverse of your lordships request'.

Despite his considerable secular power in the city, the bishop had no spiritual jurisdiction there. The city was within the Dean's peculiar so the parish churches made their presentments to the Dean and those guilty of immorality or failure to attend church were prosecuted in his court. Even today only the records of the dean and chapter are kept in the Cathedral Archives while those of the bishop are held in the County Record Office in its capacity as diocesan record office.

John Scory was appointed bishop when Elizabeth came to the throne. He was not a popular choice. Originally he had been a Dominican friar who converted to Protestantism and married when Edward VI came to the throne. When Mary re-established Catholicism, he renounced his wife and reform, but then fled to Germany, joined the Marian exiles and reverted to Protestantism. He was not happy in Hereford where he found all the canons 'dissemblers and rank papists and the Vicars choral, deacons and sextons all mortal enemies to this reformed religion. The canons will neither preach, read homilies nor minister to the holy communion nor do anything to command, beautify, or set forward this religion, but mutter against it, receive and maintain its enemies'.

Of the council of Hereford he said `there is not one that is counted favourable to this religion'. He complained to Lord Burleigh, Elizabeth's chief minister, that the mayor Mr Harvard J.P. and Master Scudamore ` protected and feted the enemies of the truth driven out of other places especially Devon'.[176] Even his plans to improve the bishop's palace so that he could live there were thwarted when he had already engaged his workmen.

Scory died in 1585 and was succeeded by Herbert Westfaling, a descendant of German immigrants. He was more popular with the chapter but still failed in an attempt to carry out a visitation of the cathedral. Bishop Bennett found the diocese `full of recusants and traditionalists' and Godwin, his successor gave up trying to influence the dean and chapter and left cathedral affairs to them. He retired to study in his palace at Whitbourne

The Reformation receives very little mention in either the act books of the Dean and Chapter or the Vicars Choral. The Dean and Chapter noted in 1550 that altars were to be replaced by tables but nothing about arranging for it to be done. However the clergy throughout the diocese obviously entered into marriage with enthusiasm as in 1554 at the beginning of Mary's reign, the act book lists a number of clergy, including four prebends, who were summoned for being married but did not attend, so were deprived.

An entry for 1553 demonstrates a rather cavalier attitude towards the parishioners of the benefices which the chapter had to provide incomes for the residentiary canons. `All future appointments in the gift of the Dean and Chapter shall be determined by a draw of wax pellets carried out by the residentiaries each having the right to present to the particular benefice which he has drawn. He may present himself or through an intermediary'[177]

A very real cause for concern on the part of the national government was the threat posed by religious extremism. After the change to Protestantism during Edward's reign followed by the return to Catholicism under Mary when over three hundred martyrs were burnt, often in their local market place, Elizabeth was anxious that her church settlement should be all –embracing. She did not 'wish to make windows into men's souls' and hoped that if her religious settlement steered a middle course the extremists would lose influence. Unfortunately, this was not to be, Protestants like Bishop Scory who had fled during Mary's reign returned and expected a strict unadorned church and, while the bulk of the population accepted the moderate changes to their local churches and were probably glad to have their services in English, a considerable minority stuck firmly to Catholicism. This situation was largely tolerated as long as they made a token gesture of going to church and did not proselytise. However, in 1570 the Pope issued the bull Regnans in Excelsis, which excommunicated Elizabeth for heresy, deprived her of her titles and absolved her subjects from their allegiance. This put Catholics in an intolerable position, forcing them to choose between their religion and their country. Most remained loyal but the presence of Mary Queen of Scots as a prisoner gave a focus to those who chose their religion, leading to a succession of plots on Elizabeth's life. At the same time, missionary priests from the continent, who came to sustain and increase the Catholic community, were perceived as an added threat, so towards the end of the century the climate had changed and the government became increasingly anxious to root them out. The catholic laity were subject to heavy fines for non-attendance at church and imprisonment or even death for harbouring a priest. The following directive is in the City records for 1586:

'By the Quene'

The Council of the Marches had heard from the Earl of Pembroke the Lord President that, 'divers persons naming themselves Jesuits and Seminaries or rather to be called massing priests have of late under colour of that their fayned religion become most wicked traytors to our state, and most hurtful poyson to our true and loving subjects. ......

We will and requier you... to cause diligent search and inquiry to be made for all and every such offender...and then tapprehend and attache them soe apprehended and taken... to bring or send to our Council in our Marches with certificates of the cause... You shall doe well by all good wayes and means and policy with secrecy to put the service in execucon from tyme to tyme ... as you wilbe noted obediente to the lawes of our realme concerning the service of God and profession of true christon religion and as you tender the suretie of our persone and the comen quiet of your countrey. And as to the contrary you will answer at your extreme peril. Given under our signet at our castle of Ludlow'.[178]

In this alarmist climate suspicions were easily aroused. In 1600 the strict examination took place of the Welsh servant of a tailor and William Cowper, a stationer and bookbinder, regarding a popish ballet which the former found sealed one morning when he opened up his master's stall and took to Cowper to read for him 'who kept it in his pocket'.[179]

In 1582 their co-citizens petitioned the mayor and council; they wanted, 'all which are not favourers, obeyors and followers of the gospell,' despite persuasion from the Bishop and Sir Henry Sidney, to be disenfranchised (i.e. lose their privileges as freemen.) After this preamble, John Elliott, gentleman, who had been a councillor in 1560 and Richard Davies fishmonger, were presented by John Garnons and Symon Wolffe, churchwardens for not attending church. They were disenfranchised for recusancy.[180]

Hereford seems, however, to have managed to pass through this period of religious change without any major disturbance. If indeed the Dean and Chapter had their mills suppressed for opposiing Henry VIII's rejection of the Pope's authority they would have been happy to see the old ways restored by Mary, so Hereford escaped the burning of heretics which took place in many other market places. Bishop John Harley, appointed in Edward's reign, was deprived during Mary's reign but he escaped into obscurity while Hooper, the Bishop of Gloucester, was burnt in London. During a royal visitationin 1561 the Dean and two Canons were deprived for refusing to take the oath (of supremacy). It is not surprising that Bishop Scory found Hereford so unfavourable to the reformed religion.

The church wardens accounts show that All Saints and Saint Nicholas' churches were at least outwardly conforming to the canons of the Elizabethan church by the beginning of the seventeenth century. They had copies of the Bible and the works of Erasmus available for the parishioners to read as required by the injunctions of Edward VI. They both had sermons as St Nicholas had a book to record the preachers names in and All Saints had an hour glass fitted to the pulpit to remind the preacher to stop. All communion chalices were to be replaced by cups; both churches list a communion cup with a lid among their possessions. Saint Nicholas church was `whited' so presumably any religious paintings on the walls had been covered over.

Records for the Dean's Court[181] do not exist for the early part of the sixteenth century so it is not possible to know the level of church attendance during this disturbed period. However, those for later in the century and the early seventeenth century show that there were regular presentments of persons in each parish for not taking communion or not attending church regulalry but as very few of the names recur, it seems that most of the absences were through neglect or illnes rather than conviction. In 1591 28 parishioners of St John's were presented for not communing at Easter. Of these, eleven either had taken communion or did so when presented. Several were not summoned, only five were actually excommunicated. One name which occurred regularly from 1595 to 1608 was that of Katherine Scudamore. As we have seen, Master Scudamore was one of those unfavourable to the reformed religion complained of by Bishop Scory. Women were more likely to stay away from church because as they could legally own no property they had nothing which could be confiscated.

In the case of `Owld' Ecly in St Owens and `Goodwife Smyth in the almes house' in Bysters ward who were presented in 1605 for not attending church infirmity was the probable reason.

The conscientiousness of the church wardens could also be a factor. The churchwardens of Saint Peters, one of whom was Philip Treherne, were presented in 1608 as the church wanted glazing and paving. They wanted (lacked) the Paraphrases of Erasmus and they did not know not if all the parishioners had received communion three times. They were to present the names of those who did not.

As well as cases of non attendance at church the church courts dealt with matters of sexual immorality so became known as the `bawdy courts'. Joan Pulley of Saint Martin's was presented for so calling the Dean's court. In 1608 there were fourteen presentments for incontinency and fornication. In three of them the girl became pregnant. In one of these, Gregory Veale was presented in May for getting Juliana Hill pregnant and again in August for fornicating with her. Unfortunately for Juliana, Gregory Veale married Anne Silcocks in the following January by special licence granted on the day of the wedding so possibly her parents had made sure their daughter was not shamed in the same way. There is no record of what happened to the baby but Juliana married in Saint Peters in 1615

The usual penance for adultery and fornication was for both parties to stand in their parish church during services clad in white sheets and holding white wands. William Harrison, who had presided over the archdiocesan court at Colchester did not think this had much effect; 'Howbeit as this is counted with some either as no punishment at all to speak of or but smally regarded of the offenders, so I would wish adultery and fornication to have some sharper law. For what great smart is it to be turned out of a hot sheet into a cold..?'[182]

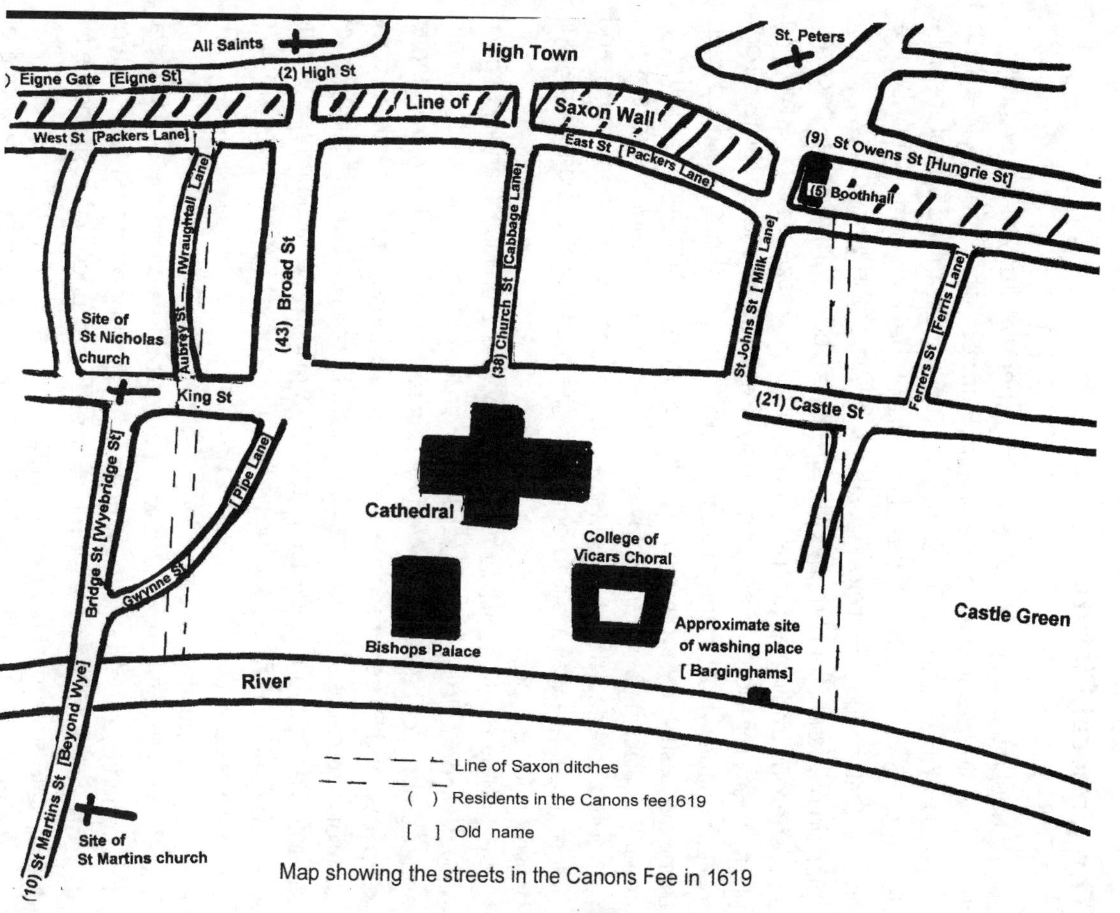

Map showing the streets in the Canons Fee in 1619

The General Picture

Although this is by no means a comprehensive study of the records for this period, it does give an impression of Hereford city during the late 16th and early 17th centuries. The suppression of the Dean and Chapter's mills did cause some hardship in the early part of the 16th century but by the end of that century Hereford, with its bustling, thrusting market place, splendid market hall and many of its streets paved, seems to have become a prosperous trading centre peopled by vigorous citizens who usually had plenty to say for themselves. It obviously drew traders and customers from Wales and the whole of the marches, as the efforts of the city guilds to keep them out testify. By today's standards the city was dirty and unhealthy; at times even lacking a water supply but this was not for want of effort by the authorities to keep the streets clean. The citizens were often rowdy and violent and there was a fair amount of crime but they also made generous provision for the poor.

Presiding over this vibrant community was a group of families which provided councillors, churchwardens, wardens of the trade guilds, sheriffs and members of parliament. With no regular police force they struggled to keep law and order, regulate the many alehouses, enforce their price controls and make sure no one who might become a burden on the poor rates could establish residence in the city while at the same time ensuring that provision was made for their poorer citizens. In addition, they had to try to enforce national regulations sent to them either directly from the Privy Council or through the Council of the Marches. Although Hereford was not directly affected, these were difficult times when the country was threatened by rebellion from Roman Catholic supporters of Mary, Queen of Scots, and later with invasion by Spain. The council was responsible for watching for potential troublemakers.

By and large these leading families seem to have dealt fairly with their fellow citizens. There were examples of favours given to leading citizens such as Thomas Church being allowed to make his door through the town wall and Widemarsh money paying for paving outside Mr Hurdman's door but as power was the only reward for their work these were trivial matters. There were inevitably complaints of partial dealing by the mayor such as this petition from Richard Hopkins and his wife Anne of Litley against his wrongful imprisonment and eviction into the street by the Vicars Choral and confiscation of their sheep. They claimed the vicars had used their influence with the mayor and council.[183]

Adding to the general bustle was the considerable number of clergy and the servants of the cathedral going about their business affairs and sometimes, it seems, as rowdy and drunken as the towns people. Certainly from their records there is no evidence that they lent an air of piety to the city streets.

Appendix I

Old and New Currency
The currency in use at this time was used up until 1970 when we went over to decimal coinage. The constant in the two systems is the pound.

`Old' Money £ 1 = 240 Pence (d.) or 20 shillings

`New' Money £ 1 = 100 New Pence (p)

One new penny = 2 . 4 d

Five new pence = One shilling

Two and a half new pence =Six pence

Twelve and a half new pence = Half–a-crown = two shillings and sixpence.

The mark, worth thirteen shillings and eight pence (66.6p) and the noble, worth six shillings and four pence (33.3p) were becoming obsolete but their use is reflected in the number of payments such as fines and rents which were set at these amounts.

Appendix 2

Glossary of Weapon Names

Almain-rivets	-flexible light armour,made of overlapping plates sliding on rivets
Brigandine-	body armour composed of iron rings or small thin iron plates sewn on canvas, linen or leather, and covered with similar materials.
Caliver	light musket, fired without a rest.
Corslet	armour covering the body.
Chamber	a detached charge piece put into the breech of a gun.
Doodging haft	boxwood dagger handle
Flash,flask	case of leather or metal to hold gun-powder
Halberd, halbert	a combination of spear and battle-axe,on a handle 5-7 feet long.
Harquebus, arquebus (arga boshes)	a portable gun supported on a rest
Jack	a sleeveless tunic or jacket, for foot soldiers usually of quilted leather, later often plated with iron
Morion (morriames)	kind of helmet without face guard or visor.
Moyen (morren ?)-	a kind of small cannon.
Sallet	light round helmet, with or without a visor, the lower part curved out at the back.
Skull (skool)	skull-cap of metal or other hard material.
Splints-	plates or strips of overlapping metal, used to protect the elbows.

Index

Bibliography

A Short History Of Hereford School ~ W. T. Carless 1914
A Description Of England William Harrison ~ ed. F.J.Furnival 1876
The Story Of Hereford ~ J and M Tonkin
Ancient Customs Of The City Of Hereford ~ Johnson
Diocesan Histories- Hereford ~ H.W. Phillott
St. Ethelbert's Fair ~ A J Winnington Ingram T.W.N.F.C. 1957 p315
The College Of The Vicars Choral ~ Phillip Barret
The England of Elizabeth ~ A.L. Rowse
The Tudor Constitution ~ G.R.Elton 1960
Poverty and Vagrancy in Tudor England ~ John Pound 1971
The English Family 1450- 1700 ~ Ralph A. Houlbrooke 1984
History and Antiquities of the County of Hereford I ~
John Duncombe 1804
Hereford Cathedral A History ~ Ed G Aylmer and J Tiller
Local Government in Hereford ~ F.C Morgan T.W.N.F.C. 1942 p37
The Government of Hereford in the Sixteenth Century ~
I.M.Slocombe T.W.N.F.C 1972 p356
The Pubs of Herford ~ Ron Shoesmith Logaston Press
The Manuscripts of Rye and Hereford Corporations ~
Historic Manuscripts Commission
Cathedral Church of Hereford ~ J. T. Bannister 1924
An Historical Account of the City of Hereford ~ John Price 1796
The Royal Charters of the City of Hereford ~ E.M. Jancey 1973
Historic Towns ~ D. Lobel 1963
The Itinerary of John Leland in about the Years 1535-43 Vol V ed Toulmin Smith

1 Abbreviations
BV = The transcriptons of records in bound volumes,
Sacks = the transcriptions of those originally stored in sheepskin sacks
HRO=Herefordshire Record Office
HCA= Hereford Cathedral Library

The City

2 Sacks 8-14 p64
3 Ibid p278
4 BV p154
5 Sacks 8-14 p126
6 Ibid p9
7 HRO BG11/10 p304
8 HCA 7003/1/1 p10

Widemarsh

9 Duncomb History and Antiquities of the County of Hereford I
10 Johnson Ancient Customs of the Sity of Hereford p155 (Johnson)
11 Sacks 16-19 p9
12 Sacks 8-14 p193
13 Sacks 16-19 p48
14 Sacks 8-14 p 271
15 BV p110
16 HRO BG11/10 p321
17 Duncomb p411/12
18 HRO BG 11/25/22
19 Sacks 8-14 p106

The Common Council

20 HRO BG11/10 p305
21 BV p66
22 Johnson p115
23 Slocombe T.W.N.F.C 1972 p356-72
24 Sacks 16-19 p91
25 BV p6
26 Rowse The England of Elizabeth p289
27 Sacks 8-14 p71
28 BV p54

Control of the People

29 John Pound Poverty and Vagrancy in Tudor England p32
30 BV p22

31 Sacks 8-14 p38
32 Ibid p69
33 Sacks 8-14 p150/154
34 Ibid p252
35 Sacks 16-19 p81
36 Sacks 8-14 p284
37 BV p87
38 Sacks 8-14 p269
39 The Manuscripts of Rye and Hereford Corporations Historic Manuscripts Commission p340 (Hereford mss)
40 BG11/10 p27

The Poor

41 A Description Of England William Harrison
42 Sacks 8-14 p390
43 HRO AG81/22
44 HRO BC63/1
45 Sacks 16-19 p119
46 Ibid p124
47 BV p94
48 Ibid p84
49 Sacks 8-14 p50
50 Prices Hereford 1796
51 Hereford mss p326
52 Sacks 8-14 p304
53 HCA 3941
54 Sacks 8-14 p252

Regulation of the Market

55 Hereford mss p326
56 BV p40
57 Ibid p30
58 Ibid p24
59 Sacks 8-14 p283
60 Sacks 16-19 p119
61 Ibid p173
62 Ibid p103
63 BV p26
64 Ibid p78
65 Ibid p82
66 Ibid p83

67 HRO BG11/10 p72
68 BV p50
69 Sacks 8-14 p289
70 Ibid p153 & 268
71 Johnson p115
72 Hereford mss p337
73 Sacks 8- 14 p118

Governement of the City

74 BV p115
75 Sacks 16-19 p59
76 BV p103
77 Ibid p20
78 Ibid p30
79 Ibid p89
80 Sacks 8-14 p23
81 BV p127
82 Ibid p26
83 Ibid p29
84 Sacks 8-14 p322
85 Ibid p282
86 Ibid p93
87 Sacks 8-14 p32
88 Ibid p19
89 Ibid p26
90 Ibid p69
91 Sacks 16-19 p119
92 Sacks 8-14 p32
93 Ibid p69
94 Ibid p19
95 Sacks 16-19 p72

Plague

96 BV p172
97 Hereford mss p328
98 HCA 7031/3
99 BV p13
100 Ibid p88
101 HCA 858/1/1
102 Hereford mss p34

Fire

103 Johnson p99-100
104 Custom Book fol4
105 Herford mss p331
106 BV p101
107 Sacks 16-19 p6
108 Sacks 8-14 p309

Defence of the Realm

109 Sacks 16-19 p104
110 Hereford mss p330
111 Sacks 16-19 p319
112 Johnson p108
113 Ibid p109
114 Morgan TWNFC 1942 p147
115 Phillott p189-190
116 Hereford Mss p335
117 Johnson p111

Women

118 De Republica Anglorem Sir Thomas Smith
119 HRO BG11/17/4
120 BV p9
121 Sacks 16-19 p81
122 HRO BC/63/1
123 Sacks 16-19 p100
124 Johnson p36
125 Sacks 16-19 p114
126 Guide to the Old House by Kathrine Willson
127 Sacks 8-14 p257
128 Ibid p255
129 Ibid p316
130 Ibid p32
131 Ibid p360
132 Sacks 16-19 p23
133 Sacks 8-14 191
134 HCA 7002/1/1
135 Sacks 16-19 p38
136 Sacks8-14 p350
137 Ibid p284
138 Ibid p270

Men

139 Ibid p23
140 Sacks 16-19 p323
141 Sacks 8-14 p348
142 Ibid p331
143 Sacks 16-19 p73
144 Ibid p93
145 Sacks 16-19 p128
146 Ibid p107
147 BV p48
148 Hereford mss p333
149 Sacks 8-14 p230
150 Sacks 16-19 p103
151 BV p85
152 Sacks 8-14 p155

Schooling

153 HCA 64
154 HCA 7002/1/3
155 Sacks 16-19 p81
156 Carless p4
157 Ibid p12
158 Ibid p15-18
159 HCA 7003/1/1 p97
160 Ibid p79
161 HCA 3362
162 HCA 3973
163 HCA 7003/1/1 p82
164 HCA 4573
165 Ibid
166 Sacks 8-14 p331
167 HRO BG11/2/17 Doc 23

The Parish Churches

168 HRO AG 81/22
169 HRO BC63/1
170 burials
171 Phillp Barret The College of the Vicars Choral
172 HCA 7003/1/1
173 HCA 4588

The Church

174 HRO B11/8/3 No 15
175 DCA
176 Bannister The Cathedral Church Of Hereford p182.
177 HCA 7031/1 fol 117r
178 BV p45
179 Ibid p41
180 Hereford Mss p338
181 HCA 7002/1/3
182 William Harrison A Description of England

The General Picture

183 BV p90